YOUR HeartSong Journey

DISCOVERING AND LIVING YOUR INSPIRED DREAM AND GOD-DESIGNED PURPOSE

GAIL ARMATYS

Publisher: HeartSong Press

ISBN: 978-1-7353075-0-3

Library of Congress Control Number: 2020912421

Bible references are from Tyndale's Life Application Study Bible, New Living Translation, Copyright © 2013 Tyndale House Foundation, unless otherwise noted.

Dedicated to my dad who taught me to persevere by his example and words of encouragement: *It's just another hurdle to jump.*

DEAR SEARCHING FRIEND,

If you're holding this book in your hands, I have no doubt you've been led to it by design. God often uses books to change lives. The best example is the Bible. I'm convinced he likes and uses other books as well. One in particular changed me and set my life on a new and incredible path. My prayer is that the Lord will use *Your HeartSong Journey* to transform your heart as well.

To begin, let's define what I mean by *HeartSong.* Everyone has an inspired dream and God-designed purpose. This just-for-you dream-purpose combination is your *HeartSong* and it was written on your heart long ago, before you were born. Knowing and living it is your significant and beautiful part of God's masterful composition. It's the *new life* you deep down crave, have been given, and are meant to live. It's also the only way to experience your greatest fulfillment because it's your unique and best expression of Christ's love.

As you travel this journey, you'll identify obstacles that may have kept you walking in circles or stopped you from experiencing this meant-just-for-you life. Here are examples of a few of them.

- Stress, exhaustion, resentment, and anger.
- Transition that creates uncertainty about what to do next.
- Lies you've been told and frankly, the ones you tell yourself.
- Circumstances that keep you stuck, trapped, and feeling empty.

- Complacency and comfort—boredom and acceptance of the status quo.
- Doubt, confusion, dissatisfaction, and fear of rejection, failure, and loss.
- Belief you can't, you're not good enough, it's selfish or impossible to live a dream of your own.

Each page of *Your HeartSong Journey* offers thoughtful questions and introspection to help you...

- Deepen your relationship with Christ.
- Break free from fear and poor self-image.
- Live believing you are deeply loved.
- Retrain your focus and thinking to build success.
- Take steps to live with more confidence and courage.
- Cast your inspired dream and claim your God-designed purpose.
- Map out with God the action steps he is calling you to take.

Ready to Risk

Maybe you're taking *Your HeartSong Journey* because you've hit what feels like a dead end in your relationship with God—or maybe you lack an understanding of his will, the difference you make, your purpose for being, and the impact of your life.

And maybe even though you do all, some, or at least a few of the right things you still find you're less than impressed or fulfilled. Like there's something missing...like you're meant for more.

Sometimes this awareness is described as feeling empty, lost, trapped, or boxed-in. And there comes a deep desire—a craving to know your significance, the mystery of why you're here, and what legacy you're meant to leave. The old life no longer satisfies. You're tired of feeling discontent or unhappy and you've come to the place where you're desperate for change. Now, you're ready to risk what it takes to draw closer to God and who and where he calls you to be. Now, you're ready know and live your HeartSong.

Through the thought-provoking questions Gail lovingly asks, the Holy Spirit revealed what I had not been able to see on my own.
—Catherine M., Client

I felt I had lost my identity in others' circumstances which in turn robbed me of my joy and inner peace—(Now) I can leave my fears behind as I surrender to and serve God boldly according to his will.
—Pamela S., Client

The prayer of my heart was to be healed from the brokenness resulting from a variety of issues ranging from fear to unworthiness. I cried out to God for healing, for the restoration of my soul. God directed me to HeartSong. Your HeartSong Journey, written through Gail, was healing. The end result was a newfound freedom, the releasing of fears, and the rejoicing of knowing that I am a beloved daughter of God.
—Susan H., Client

God used this tool to free me from long-held thinking habits that fueled fear and self-destruction tendencies. My mind has now been unlocked so that I can continue moving forward in the freedom God gave to me in Christ instead of walking around in circles in a mental prison. I have experienced God personally in my everyday, ordinary life for many years and prior to HeartSong, I would have assuredly declared that God loved me. But, this journey took a spotlight to an area of selfdoubt and distorted thinking that kept me from living in true freedom. I guess what I'm saying is that whether you've known Jesus for two days or twenty-five years, this process will be life- changing . . . and it will be good.

—Amy D., Client

CONTENTS

FOREWORD

You are about to be blessed beyond belief and transformed into more than you dream or imagine. God wanted you to find *Your HeartSong Journey* to take you to "the more" God has waiting for you. Thank God now for the victory dance you will enjoy with him when you complete this transformational journey. He is right beside you and Gail has beautifully laid out a rich and detailed plan as your guide.

Gail knows well what she writes. She has traveled this road herself. She has pioneered the way. It is a beautiful path. Know you can certainly trust this skilled, kind, knowledgeable and safe guide. Gail prayerfully laid out this trail that will take you to deep places of healing. You are meant to travel this road.

This is not just a surface level, skim over the top type of book. If you do the week-by-week, step-by-step practices and reflections set up for you, you are sure to discover and begin living the new life God intended for you at the end of your twelve weeks and beyond. This book is a practical and safe place to start your journey. You will surely find freedom you never dreamed possible.

I believe Gail's book is a beautiful key to unlocking the way for you. God desires greatly for you to be living in freedom and experiencing His love, peace, and joy. "Yet I am confident I will see the Lord's goodness while I am here in the land of the living." For us to individually declare this Psalm 27:13 as true in our own lives, we must take the first step towards his goodness. He has beautiful plans for you, dear one. It will take time and determination and pruning.

You may be watching your friends live in this goodness of the Lord and thinking you will never get to live there yourself. My dear one, yes, you can. This book will guide you to this place. Believe it and do the work.

Use this divinely inspired guide and discover the new life God has waiting for you as your inspired dream and God-design purpose begins to unfold. God is with you. You are not alone. God is cheering you on. These steps are proven and Gail is a trusted guide to unveil them. Don't skip over a step. Take the time to come away with the Beloved and He will show you secrets to your own beautiful and holy HeartSong. You are safe. You are brave. You can do this. Take the next step. Be blessed dear ones. I can hardly wait to read the testimonies of God's faithfulness to His faithful ones on your own HeartSong journey.

Sara Thurman, EdD
Author of *Small Beginnings: A Journey to the Impossible,*
and Founder of Acts 1:8 Blessings,
a ministry and art business making the name of
Jesus famous to the ends of the earth.

PROLOGUE

It was a wedding in the mountains—a destination wedding. And, oh boy, was it a climb to get there.

The hosts had everything pre-arranged for us to make the journey as simple as it could be. The path and the plan had all been created. The guests were to climb into a reserved shuttle that awaited us in the beautiful streets of Vail, Colorado. The shuttle was to take us to what was anticipated to be an incredible and perfect venue high into the mountains.

All dressed up and seated in the shuttle, we strapped in and the driver took off for our destination. The road curled 'round and 'round and was barely wide enough for one vehicle…never mind many times cars and buses were coming down the mountain from the other direction. *Gulp*. Still, our personal driver always did what was necessary to keep us safe—he'd stop, move forward, or make way by moving aside.

Did I mention the drop-off on my side of the shuttle on the way up? *Don't look, don't look* was all I could think. But, there was no need to worry. The driver knew what he was doing. And, there wasn't much he could change about the condition of the road. Yes, it was washboard rough. No matter. The hike up that road was a necessary part of the journey if we wanted to get to our planned destination.

Once we arrived and stepped out of the shuttle, all we saw were rustic cabins and a gravel parking lot. Really, is this it? So, we walked our way over a little rise and there it was. The view we'd been anticipating. Suddenly, it was obvious why the bride and groom picked this exact spot for their wedding.

Spread before us was a picture post-card only God could have painted—a peaceful lake in a sunken valley with the greens and browns of fall just settling in. A couple of people were fly-fishing. Some canoeing and another paddle boarding. On the other side of the lake were moose wading in and out of the water. And, there was a trail that disappeared into the woods—around and up the majestic mountain.

It was breathtaking, magical, and so worth the ride. But the truth is the long, scary, bumpy trip we took to get there wasn't only about a beautiful, perfect, dream-like spot for a wedding; it was about the anticipation and excitement of the journey we experienced and had to take to see a new life beginning.

Your journey to discovering God's dream and purpose for your life is similar to the story of this destination wedding. Yes, you'll have high expectations, exhilarating moments, turns, potential drop-offs, and maybe a bumpy road or two as you navigate your way. But, always, always your driver knows where he is taking you and isn't rattled by anything along your personal trail.

And if you stay the course and let him lead, you'll experience all he claimed long ago especially for you.

HOW TO USE THIS WORKBOOK AND GUIDE

Your HeartSong Journey is a three-step roadmap that guides you to discover more of the true you, more of Christ in you, and your pre-determined and divine destination—the unique mission God has in mind just for you. As you go along, you'll learn how you can break through the things that hold you back and keep you stuck so you can walk your especially appointed journey with the peace, confidence, and joy Christ has already deposited in you.

Like any trail you walk, you must keep putting one foot in front of the other and do the work to get up the path. No one can take this journey for you. And yes, it takes daring, desire, time, and commitment. But I assure you, if you're ready to draw closer to Christ and discover your HeartSong—if you're ready to take a chance and move up and on to your most meaningful and fulfilling life, then you're absolutely in the right place.

What to Expect

On this journey, you will first and foremost discover God has never left your side…*ever*. And as God moves this knowledge from your head to your heart, my hope is you'll allow yourself to be lavished in his love—deepening your personal relationship with every prayer you whisper, scripture you read, question you ask and answer, and each page you turn.

And just so you know, if your journey is to be successful, you'll need to do more than read. You'll find as you go you have heart work to complete. The introspective questions and bible-based guidance helps you prepare to live out your calling. As you would expect, this will take time and thoughtful consideration. But it's so worth it because it's your chance to discover and share the deep longings of your heart with Christ. And his with you.

Your journey includes three steps.

Step One   <u>Discovering Your True Identity and Sacred Worth</u>
Good Enough—Loved No Matter What

Step Two   <u>Breaking Free from What Holds You Back</u>
Overcoming Obstacles—Building Character

Step Three <u>Casting Your Dream. Claiming Your Purpose. Taking Action.</u>
Moving Forward as God Leads

Each step of your journey is marked with life-changing *Heart Challenges*. These challenges include a short story, scriptures, questions, assessments, and other helps to move you forward.

Your Roadmap

Here are a few tips to help you begin and complete this journey.

> ➤ I recommend you walk this journey with your coach, friend, or in a small group setting so you can designate an accountability partner to keep you on track. Be sure to finish each assigned *Heart Challenge* prior to meeting so you can best experience the revelation the Holy Spirit has in mind for you and discuss your responses and experiences together. Be willing to ask and answer difficult questions of yourself.*

> ➤ Plan up to twelve weeks to complete this journey. And be intentional to work through each Heart Challenge in sequence before moving on; they're meant to be cumulative.

> ➤ To help you keep moving forward, be accountable to one another. Encourage and pray for each other. Be *deliberate* and *disciplined* about setting aside time to complete your Heart Challenges rather than hoping to squeeze time in at some random point during your day.

> ➤ Investing your time in this journey with Christ should be one of your top priorities. This isn't meant to be just one more thing to add to your to-do list. God wants you to draw near to him not run to catch up! Make and take time. Linger with the Lord and meditate on what he teaches you as you complete each challenge.

---

* This journey may be taken alone but finding a coach, friend, or small group to walk with you is recommended. Sharing your journey helps keep you from hurrying through, straggling behind, or veering off track so you don't miss all God has in store for you.

➢ As you've probably realized, this isn't a traditional Bible study, but you'll want your Bible by your side as you go along. Since God has created all, knows all, and understands all—including everything about you, it seems wise to go to him for answers and direction.

➢ Lastly, to create your best and most transformational experience, decide now you will be transparent, vulnerable, and prayerful along this deeply personal journey so you can receive the life-giving insight God has in mind just for you!

Stop struggling uphill. Lean into Jesus on your journey. Ask him to give you a glimpse of his vision for your life. Let him get you to your destination. It's just over the rise. And it's there, you'll discover the beautiful song written on your heart long ago. The one you're meant to live for his glory, your greatest fulfillment and the benefit of others.

STEP ONE

Discovering Your True Identity and Sacred Worth

Good Enough—Loved No Matter What

Like any journey, this one must have a starting point. *Your HeartSong Journey* begins by stepping into the knowledge and application of your sacred worth—the truth that declares you are good enough because Christ is enough. In Christ you are chosen. You are accepted. You are loved…no matter what.

Viewing yourself in the mirror of this truth is the right place to start. Because discovering who you *really* are (not what someone told you or you've chosen to believe) changes the way you think, the choices you make, the depth of your relationships, the enjoyment of your life, and your legacy.

STEP ONE: DISCOVERING YOUR TRUE IDENTITY
AND SACRED WORTH

Define yourself radically as one beloved by God.
This is the true self. Every other identity is illusion.

—Brennan Manning

HEART CHALLENGE 1

Identifying Your Current Life Scenario

Everyone is of sacred value.
You are made for more because you are worth more.
You have the image of Christ stamped on you.

—Ben Trammell

How Do You See Yourself?

Below are six scenarios describing familiar thoughts and feelings. Read the following instructions and determine which, if any, of the descriptions in the scenarios fit how you see yourself completely or in part.[1]

- Circle the scenario(s) that seem to apply to you most. *(More than one may apply.)*
- Underline individual words in each description that resonate with you.
- If you don't see yourself in these scenarios and their descriptions, write your own using the space provided at the end.

Which Scenario Best Describes You?

Confused

- I'm at a loss about what to do next.
- I know I have gifts to offer but I just don't know how to unleash my talents and abilities.
- I need clarity. I'm not sure of God's will for my life.

Stuck

- There are things I want to do, mountains for me to climb, and people for me to serve, but I can't seem to gain any momentum.
- I have a dream for my life, but I don't know how to accomplish it.
- I feel frustrated, trapped, paralyzed in my circumstances.

Out-of-Balance

- I'm clear on my dream and purpose. I'm just so busy I can't keep up.
- My family and friendships are suffering.
- I feel tense, stressed, and sometimes—maybe too often—resentful and angry.
- I need to find peace in my life. I'm exhausted. Overwhelmed.

Dissatisfied

- I have a good life, but for some reason, I'm unhappy and maybe even a bit bored.
- I know something is missing, but what?

- I have a sense of emptiness and feel like I'm meant for more.
- I'm dissatisfied even though I really do have a good life.

Afraid

- I know I need to make a change, but it seems risky and I'm comfortable where I am.
- I like being in control and the thought of not knowing exactly what's going to happen if I try something new or different scares me.
- I might look incompetent, fail, or create more work for myself if I try.
- I want to believe I can but struggle with fear and doubt.

Livin' the Dream

- I'm thankful for my life. I know my unique purpose and live with intention. I wake up in the morning looking forward to doing things I enjoy, learning and challenging myself, serving, and knowing I make a difference.

Write your own scenario

_____

_____

_____

_____

_____

_____

_____

_____

What thoughts do you have about what you've written? What jumps out at you most?

_____

_____

_____

What Do You Want God to Do?

In 2 Chronicles 1:7, God asks Solomon, *What do you want?* Likewise, we find in Mark 10:51, Jesus inquires of the blind beggar: *What do you want me to do for you?*

Clearly, God is pleased to hear our specific requests.

Knowing this and the scenario you're currently living, give your response to Jesus's question: *What do you want me to do for you as together we walk Your HeartSong Journey?*

_____

_____

_____

_____

_____

_____

_____

As you move through this journey, remember to praise and worship the Lord. Share your heart with him and let him share his heart with you. Answer his question about what you want him to do for you before you complete each Heart Challenge—always listening for and expecting his response.

HEART CHALLENGE 2

Who Do You Say You Are?

We never know who we really are
until we invite Christ in.

—John Stephenson

Matthew 16:13–16 tells us Jesus walked with his disciples and asked them, "Who do people say the Son of Man is?"

They replied, "Some say John the Baptist; others say Elijah; and still others, Jeremiah or one of the prophets."

Jesus asked, "But what about you? Who do you say I am?"

Then Peter responded, "You are the Messiah, the Son of the living God."

Jesus often used the art of asking a question to teach. It seems in this case, Jesus wanted to confirm in the disciples' own minds that he was far more than what the people had to say. So, he asked who *they* said he was.

Jesus knew then and now that when we speak something aloud we gain understanding. Peter boldly stated Jesus is "the Messiah, the Son of the living God."

Peter believed.

What about you? Who do you say Jesus is? (Use whatever words come to mind.)

_____

_____

_____

Who Do You Say You Are?

Now, let's take Jesus's question, turn it inward, and answer the following:

Who do you say you are?

- Use the space provided on the following page to write out your answer. It can be as long or short as you desire. Include your perceptions of your personality, talents, preferences, strengths, and weaknesses. Enjoy this exercise, and allow yourself to be thoughtful, honest, and vulnerable to the heart of the question.

Just for fun…here is my sample.

I am a woman who, in her youth, was told and believed she was too sensitive and felt "not good enough." Now I am transformed, and knowing my true identity and understanding the gift of my sensitive spirit, I am able to help others. I am the wife of a husband who loves me more than anything and tells and shows me all the time. I am blessed. I am someone who struggled greatly as a young adult, has been through a divorce, and while it devastated me, I came through it broken, better, stronger, and more forgiving, compassionate, and wiser than I went into it.

I am a mother who considers having a loving family a dream come true. I am proud of my kids and love more than anything when we are all together. I am a daughter who prays for and loves my parents. I am a sister who, though separated by miles, has gotten better at keeping in touch. I am an introvert (I gain strength from time alone) and a person who enjoys laughing and being with my friends. I am someone who can have high expectations of myself. I find encouraging and guiding others is my sweet spot. I can be impatient. I think I'm smart enough, but even more, I seek God's wisdom and discernment, and have a desire to share what I learn.

I am not too good at resting. I am an entrepreneur with both successes and failures. I am creative. I am a bit of a musician. I am a singer. I am not a hummer. I am a person who finds solace and connection with God in nature. I am an animal lover and consider cardinals God's special gift to me; I sense his love and presence when they are near. I am a learner and lover of scripture. By God's grace, I am an overcomer of an eating disorder, divorce, poor self-image, fear, doubt, and failure. I am God's child. I am chosen. I am loved.

Now, write your own answer. *Who do you say you are?*

Our lives are largely shaped
by our perception of ourselves.

—Unknown

Who do you say you are?

_____

_____

_____

_____

_____

_____

_____

_____

_____

_____

God loved us and **chose us** in Christ.

—Ephesians 1:4

Accept each other, just as **Christ has accepted you.**

—Romans 15:7

See what great **love the Father has lavished on us**,
that we should be called children of God!

—1 John 3:1 (NIV)

You are chosen.
You are accepted.
You are loved.

Heart Challenge 3

Who Does God Say You Are?

Yet, O Lord, you are our Father.
We are the clay, and you are the potter.
We all are formed by your hand.

—Isaiah 64:8

Have you heard about or read Dr. Gary Chapman's book, *The 5 Love Languages*? It's about tuning into what makes our significant others feel most loved.[2]

The five languages include words of affirmation, receiving gifts, physical touch, acts of service, and quality time. My primary love language is receiving gifts…just in case you're wondering. However, it's not my husband's. Years ago, he'd rather do almost anything than receive a gift. This seemed very odd to me![*]

Over time, though, he has learned to accept gifts by viewing the gesture as something that brings joy to the giver. By refocusing on the giver, he has come to know a gift's significance.

---

[*] Discover your love language by taking the online assessment at:
https://www.5lovelanguages.com/profile/

This makes me think about God and how he loved the idea of each of us, wanted us, created us, and so gave us the gift of life. I wonder, do you find meaning in this uniquely wrapped gift of your life? Do you know your significance? Do you know your sacred worth?

Is it time for you to refocus on the Giver of your life, the One to whom you belong?

You belong to your Creator—your Father. Who does *he* say you are?

Who Does God Say You Are?

To gain a better perspective of your sacred worth, read below who God, your Creator *(the One who made you)* and Father *(the One who loves you)*, says you are.

- See what great love the Father has lavished on us, that we should be called children of God! And that is what we are! 1 John 3:1 (NIV)

You are God's child—heir to the King.

- So if the Son sets you free, you are truly free. John 8:36

You are free.

- Don't you realize your body is the temple of the Holy Spirit? 1 Corinthians 6:19

You are sacred.

- I can do everything through Christ who gives me strength. Philippians 4:13

You are strong and able.

- There is no condemnation for those who belong to Christ Jesus. Romans 8:1

You are not condemned. You are forgiven.

- My old self has been crucified with Christ. It is no longer I who live, but Christ lives in me. Galatians 2:20

You are a new creation—a reflection of Christ.

- Nothing can ever separate us from God's love. Romans 8:38–39

You are loved—no matter what and always.

- God causes everything to work together for the good of those who love him and are called according to his purpose for them. Romans 8:28

God's plans for you are good—you were created for a purpose.

- God is faithful. He will not allow the temptation to be more than you can stand. 1 Corinthians 10:13

You can withstand temptation.

- If God is for us, who can ever be against us? Romans 8:31

God is on your side.

- With God we will gain the victory. Psalm 60:12 (NIV).

With him you are victorious!

Now, take a moment to think about what you've just learned and answer the following questions.

Are there discrepancies between who you say you are (Heart Challenge #2) and who God says you are?

If so, what are they?

_____

_____

_____

If you believe God is your Creator and Father, what words can you use to describe who you are in his eyes?

_____

_____

_____

Do you believe it?

_____

_____

_____

Do you live like you believe it?

_____

_____

_____

What changes will you make in your day-to-day living and thinking to live more like you believe you are who God says you are?

_____

_____

_____

God is asking you to believe who he says he is,
believe who he says you are,
then live like you believe those things.

—Unknown

God loved the idea
of each of us, wanted us,
created us, and so gave us
the gift of life.

HEART CHALLENGE 4

Chosen, Not Compared

You didn't choose me. I chose you.

—John 15:16

We learn at a young age that life is competitive. To be chosen for the playground soccer team, the spelling bee, and the high school band—to get the job, keep the job, and get the promotion—in order to win the vote, the nod, and the accolades—we must prove ourselves to be good enough.

Sometimes, we succeed; and, sometimes we fall short. When we don't meet our goal and expectations (or maybe someone else's), get the position, or win the prize, it can hurt. We may feel defeated—again.

When this happens, it's not uncommon to hear a familiar voice reminding us we don't measure up. Often, the source of this voice is comparison. Comparison is dangerous and can swiftly become the lie *I'm not good enough.*

Lies, in general, are plenty bad. But inward-focused lies that keep you and me from stepping into the waters we are called to cross are life diminishing. The resulting feeling is inadequacy.

Can you describe one of the first times you felt you were not good enough? Inadequate? Briefly recall the situation.

_____

_____

_____

How do you think this experience may have impacted your life?

_____

_____

_____

We wouldn't dare say that we are as wonderful as these other men who tell you how important they are! But they are only comparing themselves with each other, using themselves as the standard of measurement. How ignorant!

—2 Corinthians 10:12

Need to Be Known

I have two older sisters. Growing up, my oldest sister, by five years, was my idol! I thought she was so pretty and I wanted to be just like her. In my eyes, she hung the moon—even though I recall she often tired of me following her and her friends around crying out from time to time, *Mouuuummm! Gail won't leave us alone!*

The sister closest to my age was smart and social and the one I fought with frequently. Yes, sad to say—scratching, pinching, pulling hair fights! I cringe at the admission. Of course, we also had many fun times and are dear friends.

By the time I got to high school, the success of both of my sisters preceded me. The teachers knew I was their little sister, but somehow, they couldn't remember I had a first name of my own. Oh, the trials of being the baby of the family.

My parents had difficulty remembering my name, too! Of course, now I can totally relate based on my confusion when calling my own kids' names! It wasn't just about my namelessness; my comparison was with everything about them that brought them attention and others joy. All I really wanted was to be known for being me. Wasn't I good enough? I didn't think so.

We have a need to be known. Not just known about. Known. Do you feel known? Please explain.

_____

_____

_____

Read Psalm 139:1–18. You might already know this scripture. But, please, take time to read it now. In fact, read it aloud! Hearing God's word is good for the soul. How do God's words encourage you?

_____

_____

_____

What comparisons have you made in the past that led you to belittle yourself, your abilities, your value, and your uniqueness?

_____

_____

_____

Look back and record how making comparisons may have affected you, your thoughts and beliefs, and the decisions you've made as the years progressed.

_____

_____

_____

> If we don't know who we are, we'll never
> know how we ought to live.
>
> —Billy Graham

Comparison and Confidence

Comparisons can determine your level of confidence. They can lead to pride or they can lead to insecurity.

If you define your worth by measuring yourself against other people, your level of confidence will move up and down like a swing depending on whom you happen to be comparing yourself to at the time.

> You'll either think yourself worse than someone else,
> or better than someone else.
> Neither of these is good.
> Stop comparing.
>
> —Rick Warren

How do you think comparisons have directed your level of self-worth?

_____

_____

_____

Read John 21:15–22. Jesus reinstated Peter after his three-time denial of Christ. He asked Peter to confirm his love, commanded him to feed his sheep, follow him, and in the end, bring glory to God by his death.

The next thing we know, Peter turned to see the disciple Jesus loved following them. Peter seemed to feel threatened by the disciple's presence and asked, "Lord, what about him?" Was Peter comparing his own role, relationship with Jesus, and purpose to this disciple's?

Jesus's immediate response (v. 22) is telling of his disdain for comparison and his desire for each of us to know that because of his great love for us, he has a unique plan and purpose for each of us.

> Jesus replied, "If I want him to remain alive until I return, what is that to you? As for you, follow me!"
>
> —John 21:22

What comparisons are you making today that may be keeping you from believing and accepting God's love and fulfilling his unique plan and purpose for your life? What might be Jesus's response to your comparisons?

_____

_____

_____

Acknowledge that the Lord is God.
He made us, and we are his.

—Psalm 100:3

Comparison is dangerous
and can swiftly
become the lie
I'm not good enough.

HEART CHALLENGE 5

Always Good Enough

If only you knew how beautiful you are unconditionally.
Don't you know it's enough if all you do is breathe?

—Brittany Burgunder

Our choices often reveal our belief that we are not good enough. It's a belief born and perpetuated by shame-filled thoughts that tell us we aren't loveable, we don't belong—perhaps even that we're unforgiveable.

It wasn't until after my divorce that I began to grow in my relationship with Jesus. More specifically, it was when he spoke into my heart, *"You have to change."*

I argued with him for ten futile seconds, comparing my behavior to my ex-husband's. As if that made me better. After all, I wasn't involved in *big* sins like he was—just the everyday, ordinary kind. I was a nice person and cared about doing the right things, but I knew my argument was weak. I was convicted. I had to change.

I didn't always recognize my wrong choices as sin, nor did I understand the influence this had on my life and the lives of others. I had not considered my fear, doubt, and false humility sin. I didn't know they were stumbling blocks to living my best life.

And I didn't realize my lack of self-worth was a pivot many of my sins could grab hold of and swing around.

After my 'come to Jesus' encounter and a long, dry spell in our relationship, I began to read my Bible and spend time alone with God. His words comforted me and revealed there was nothing I had done in the past—nothing I could do in the future—that would or could keep God from loving me.

He had already loved me to death—literally—by sacrificing his Son for my sins.

What greater expression of love is there? What more could be given on my behalf?

I began to understand: by Jesus's sacrifice, my worth became sacred. So did yours.

To live fully you must, every moment, every day, *choose to believe* there is nothing you can do or strive to be that will cause you to be loved and accepted more than God has already loved and accepted you.

There is no achievement you can gain or human praise you can receive that validates your worth more than Jesus's sacrifice does. There is no human failure, wrong, or violation big or bad enough to take away what has already been given.

Christ's sacrificial, blood-laden love proves your sacred worth.

Am I good enough? No. Not on my own. Neither are you. The only thing that makes us good enough is God's love pouring out through Jesus's sacrifice and into our very being.

By the way, he made this sacrifice on your behalf long ago. So, any error you make, shame you feel, insufficiency you find in your actions and yourself cannot rightly claim *I am not good enough.* Because the Creator of heaven and earth, you and me—everything— has already pronounced through Christ that you are.

It's a done deal.

How does knowing your good enough-ness doesn't come from your attempts to do right, be better or perfect, be known and accepted, make more money or have more stuff change the way you regard yourself?

_____

_____

_____

Do you believe your good enough-ness comes only from the One who thought you worthy of his death? If so, what old beliefs and actions does this require you to change? If not, how and where do you find your value?

_____

_____

_____

In our search for significance, it's worth everything to remember: nothing and no one but God gives us our identity and self-worth. Anything else we try replaces him in our lives. We are free, called, and meant to live fulfilling and purposed lives, but we are not free to replace God.

Anyone who trusts in him will never be put to shame.

—Romans 10:11 (NIV)

Christ's sacrificial,
blood-laden love
proves your
sacred worth.

HEART CHALLENGE 6

Self-Love

I have loved you with an everlasting love; I
have drawn you with loving kindness.

—Jeremiah 31:3 (NIV)

You know about God's top ten list of commandments, right? Do
you remember what Jesus said when he was asked by the expert in
religious law which commandments were the top two?

You must love the Lord your God with all your heart,
all your soul, and all your mind. This is the first
and greatest commandment. A second is equally
important: Love your neighbor as yourself.

—Matthew 22:37–39

1. Love the Lord your God.
2. Love your neighbor as yourself.

Could the message to the expert and to us be that our love for our neighbor and ourselves is an extension and expression of our love for God? If so, Jesus's answer is life-changing.

The Lord tells us loving God is the first and greatest commandment. Then he says the second is equally important. We are to love our neighbor *as* (similar to) the love we have for ourselves. *Not only is our ability to love others an extension and expression of our love for God, it's at the same time directly related to the love we have for ourselves.* How do we love others if we don't love ourselves? May I suggest, not well?

And get this… Jesus says, in John 15:12, *Love each other in the same way I have loved you.* Now, we can add on to the previous statement:

Our love for our neighbor is an extension and expression of our love for God and is directly related to the love we have for ourselves but first—it's an extension and expression of God's love for us.

We love each other because he loved us first.

—1 John 4:19

And, he expresses his love in action.

For God so loved the world, he gave his only begotten Son.

—John 3:16 (KJV)

Once we accept God's love through Christ, we can and are meant to love ourselves and express that same love—Christ's love—to others. Make sense?

But here's the not-so surprising kicker. If we listen to the world, we hear two extremes regarding self-love.

1. Of course, you should love yourself and put yourself first above everyone else. Who matters more than you?
2. If you love yourself, you are being selfish, prideful, and conceited. Everyone matters more than you.

Despite what the world may say, you are *commanded* to love yourself, how God made you, and who he made you to be—when you do, you can fully love others. Love is a command not a suggestion!

At the risk of applying an over-used metaphor, think of it as putting your oxygen mask on first as they drop from the ceiling of the bouncing airplane. *(I hope you never experience this!)* If you don't do this, how can you best help those around you? Likewise, if you are to live fully, you must be able to help those around you. And to best help those around you, you must believe you are sacred to God. He's got a reason for you to be here. He chose you. He made you. He loves you.

What's not to love?

Your looks? Your hair, voice, height? Your mistakes, regrets, sins, defeats? God doesn't see you through the lens of shame and self-inflicted criticism. God sees you as his beloved child. He sees you through Christ.

Set aside any thoughts or claim to ego. This is not God's desire for you. But, what you must believe is that you and I reflect and share God's goodness and love for others to the extent we accept it from God and in ourselves.

Will you hear and believe this truth? Will you breathe in God's life-giving love? Will you choose to accept his transforming love and love who he made you to be? As you do, you will glorify God, share his love with others, and experience greater joy.

How do we begin to love ourselves so we can love our neighbors? We start by asking and answering the question: *What is love?*

This is love:

Love is patient, love is kind. It does not envy, it does not boast,
it is not proud. It is not rude, it is not self-seeking, it is not
easily angered, it keeps no record of wrongs. Love does not
delight in evil but rejoices with the truth. It always protects,
always trusts, always hopes, always perseveres. Love never fails.

—1 Corinthians 13:4–8 (NIV)

Let's take a look at your current self-love tendencies based not
on the world's definition of love, but on God's. On a scale of 1–10,
1 is *low or no*, 10 is *high or yes*. Indicate the number that best reflects
your life today.

- Love is patient.

Are you patient with yourself?

|--|
 1   2   3   4   5   6   7   8   9   10

- Love is kind.

Are you kind to yourself?

|--|
 1   2   3   4   5   6   7   8   9   10

- Love does not envy.

Is there someone you envy?

|--|
 1   2   3   4   5   6   7   8   9   10

- Love does not boast.

Do you boast about yourself?

```
|-----------------------------------------------------------|
 1    2    3    4    5    6    7    8    9    10
```

- Love is not proud.

Do you catch yourself being prideful? Note: False humility is a form of pride.

```
|-----------------------------------------------------------|
 1    2    3    4    5    6    7    8    9    10
```

- Love is not rude.

Do you speak mean-spirited things to yourself?

```
|-----------------------------------------------------------|
 1    2    3    4    5    6    7    8    9    10
```

- Love is not self-seeking.

Do you live to serve others?

```
|-----------------------------------------------------------|
 1    2    3    4    5    6    7    8    9    10
```

- Love is not easily angered.

Are you easily angered with yourself?

```
|-----------------------------------------------------------|
 1    2    3    4    5    6    7    8    9    10
```

- Love keeps no record of wrongs.

Have you forgiven yourself for past choices or mistakes?

|--|
  1   2   3   4   5   6   7   8   9   10

- Love does not delight in evil but rejoices with the truth.

Are there lies you believe about yourself?

|--|
  1   2   3   4   5   6   7   8   9   10

- Love always protects, trusts, hopes, and perseveres.

Do you protect yourself from harm? What you see, what you hear, whom you hang out with, what you eat, what you think, what you do…?

|--|
  1   2   3   4   5   6   7   8   9   10

Do you trust the Holy Spirit in you?

|--|
  1   2   3   4   5   6   7   8   9   10

Are you hopeful?

|--|
  1   2   3   4   5   6   7   8   9   10

Do you persevere in difficulty?

|--|
1   2   3   4   5   6   7   8   9   10

- Love never fails.

Do you easily give up on you?

|--|
1   2   3   4   5   6   7   8   9   10

What do your answers reveal about your level of self-love today?

_____

_____

_____

How can you fully impact your world and love your life if you don't humbly love and care for yourself?

_____

_____

_____

How does knowing *God is love* (1 John 4:8) and that his Spirit *lives in you* (1 Corinthians 3:16) affect your concept and acceptance of self-love?

_____

_____

_____

Will you believe and accept the transforming love of Christ? How might this change your love for self and your neighbor?

_____

_____

_____

If we pray, we will believe;
If we believe, we will love;
If we love, we will serve.

—Mother Teresa

God sees you as his beloved child.

HEART CHALLENGE 7

Lavished in Love, Not Pride or Shame

Shame is the most powerful master emotion.
It's fear that we're not good enough.

—Brené Brown

In his book, *He Chose the Nails*, Max Lucado refers to pride and shame as "sisters." Unlikely sisters—but closely related as they both work to keep us from God's love.

"Pride puffs out her chest."
"Shame hangs her head."
"Pride boasts."
"Shame hides."
"Pride seeks to be seen."
"Shame seeks to be avoided."
"Pride says, *You're too good for him.*"
"Shame says, *You're too bad for him.*"
"Pride drives you away, shame keeps you away."

—Max Lucado, *He Chose the Nails*

Pride and shame are not a couple of sisters we want to or should hang out with. Unfortunately, we often do. But thankfully, in his passion for us, our "God, the sinless and selfless Father, loves us in our pride and shame."[3]

How do pride and shame keep you from believing the truth of your identity and sacred worth? How do they keep you from accepting and sharing God's love?

_____

_____

_____

Read the following verses.

Be honest in your evaluation of yourselves, measuring yourselves by the faith God has given us.

—Romans 12:3b

So now there is no condemnation for those who belong to Christ Jesus.

—Romans 8:1

How might these verses help you maintain the right perspective regarding your sacred worth?

_____

_____

_____

When ego and pride tell you you're better than and self-condemnation and shame scream you're not good enough, whom will you choose to believe and why?

_____

_____

_____

How might believing in your heart by Jesus's sacrifice you are free from shame and condemnation change your days? Your life?

_____

_____

_____

If pride is what goes before a fall,
then shame is what keeps you from getting up after one.

—Max Lucado

…by Jesus's sacrifice
you are free
from shame and
condemnation.

STEP TWO

Breaking Free from What Holds You Back

Overcoming Obstacles—Building Character

There are many obstacles to break through and hurdles to jump on our way to discovering God's destiny for our lives. Trials, losses, attitudes, people, and so many other things keep us stuck or stop us cold. The truth is, we often let those things hold us back (or maybe use them as an excuse) more than we want to admit. But what if we experienced these roadblocks along our journey differently? What if we *decide* to accept them as things that draw us closer to God and allow him to transform, develop, and strengthen our character and grow our relationship with him? What if these challenges are our road to deliverance?

Psalm 105:20 reminds us of Joseph's character-building test. *Until the time came to fulfill his dreams, the Lord tested Joseph's character.*

It seems character development is a necessary and long-standing tradition with God, and one area he simply won't let us skip past even though the pain of the passage can feel like failure. In fact, someone once said, "Failure is almost always caused by a character flaw." If that's true, what does it mean to view overcoming disappointment, hardships, challenges—the things that hold you back—as a process God uses for character development? What would change for you? The fact is; God is most interested in you and your relationship with him. So, from a heavenly perspective, you and I need (and God uses) the barriers within and before us to inspire Christ-like change. John Ortberg says it well: "God is primarily in the character-forming business, not the circumstance-shaping business."

God's desire is for your character to be strengthened in Christ. If you allow, he leads you to complete the purpose to which you are called and as you go with him, you come to realize the fulfillment and freedom found in your relationship with him. His love pours out of you. His strength becomes yours. His peace becomes yours. His words. His steps—yours.

Step two of *Your HeartSong Journey* is your opportunity to not only experience breakthrough but also to move nearer to God and pour out more of Christ as you lean into him, toward the goal God has set for you.

While character development may feel a bit like you're in the hot seat, take note: At no time does this step call for self-condemnation. Only reflection, surrender, and excitement for the good God has in mind for you.

You'll begin this part of your journey by expressing your values.

You can't go back and change the beginning,
but you can start where you are and change the ending.

—C.S. Lewis

HEART CHALLENGE 1

Your Values

It's hard not to make a decision
when you know what your values are.

—Roy Disney

When did you last take time to define your values? It's probably been a while—if ever.

We may recognize and pay attention to our values when we confront a situation that calls for a decision. But even then, we don't usually consciously consider the decisions we make are based on values we hold.

If you look back on recent choices you've made, you'll likely see, now that you're thinking about it, they were based on one or more of your values.

What do I mean by values? A value reveals your inmost sense of what is wrong and what is right. Values are a tool of discernment.

Priorities and values seem similar. It's true, they're related, and yet, they're different. *Priorities* are the way you order your life: this first, this second, this third, etc. *Values* help you determine your priorities. *I value my health, so I will prioritize it by putting exercise near the top of my list of priorities. When I wake up in the morning and don't want to exercise, the value I put on my health reminds me it is a priority and helps me decide to exercise anyway.*

Another example. If I recognize that I value family, I can more easily prioritize my family time over activities I've been invited to attend or roles and responsibilities I'm considering.

Defining your values helps you make good decisions. When your values line up with God's, and you adhere to them, you can be sure you're walking in step with him.

> Our willingness to wait reveals the value we
> place on what we're waiting for.
>
> —Charles Stanley

Read the following scriptures. What value do you believe God emphasizes most in each?

1. Jesus replied, "'You must love the Lord your God with all your heart, all your soul, and all your mind.' A second is equally important: 'Love your neighbor as yourself.'" Matthew 22:37, 39

_____

_____

_____

2. Have faith in God. Mark 11:22

_____

_____

_____

3. Humble yourself before the Lord, and he will lift you up in honor. James 4:10

_____

_____

_____

4. For we are God's masterpiece. He has created us in Christ Jesus, so we can do the good things he planned for us long ago. Ephesians 2:10

_____

_____

_____

5. But test everything that is said. Hold on to what is good. Stay away from every kind of evil. 1 Thessalonians 5:21–22

_____

_____

_____

6. But, seek first his kingdom and his righteousness, and all these things will be given to you as well. Matthew 6:33 (NIV)

_____

_____

_____

7. For God is not a God of disorder but of peace. 1 Corinthians 14:33

_____

_____

_____

8. Yet the Lord longs to be gracious to you; therefore he will rise up to show you compassion. Isaiah 30:18 (NIV)

_____

_____

_____

9. How great is the love the Father has lavished on us, that we should be called children of God! 1 John 3:1

_____

_____

_____

Now, make a list of *your* values.

_____

_____

_____

In what ways do you think your values might inspire your priorities? Your HeartSong?

_____

_____

_____

Acknowledging godly values in your life is key to knowing and living your HeartSong. Godly values help make your heart steadfast and footsteps sure along your path.

Values are like fingerprints…
You leave 'em all over everything you do.

—Elvis Presley

When your values line up with God's,
and you adhere to them,
you can be sure you're walking
in step with him.

HEART CHALLENGE 2

Your Priorities

Most of us spend too much time on what is urgent and
not enough time on what is important.
—Stephen R. Covey

Back in the day, when I drove to my office in Houston each morning, I knew my list of things to do was waiting for me. After settling in with a cup of coffee, I would do a quick review and decide which item on the list had the biggest impact on the company and the lives of those associated with it. In other words, I scheduled my priorities.

This brief evaluation nearly always led to the thing that would require the biggest investment of my resources and time. It would also often be that thing I was least eager to do but would be happy to have completed.

I set my priorities. I would do a particular thing first because it mattered most. My priorities informed the way I used my time.

Setting priorities in our lives—not only in our work—can be addressed in the same way. Have you checked what's most important and life-affecting to you and those around you lately?

If you already have a list of priorities, I urge you to use what you discover in the following exercise to review and reset them as you are inspired by the Spirit. If you aren't sure of your priorities, it's time to get them set.

- Create a list of up to five priorities. A few life categories are provided to help you get started or you can choose others of your own. Add specific intentions next to each category to help you live your priorities. (There may be some overlap of intentions in your various categories.)
- Record the outcome you desire as you live into each priority.

Prior to beginning to pray, ask God to reveal any misaligned priorities, intentions, or desired outcomes.

Life Category Samples

Work/	Family/	God/	Self/	Marriage/	Church/
Community	Travel	Hobbies	Friends	Health	Finances

Example:	**Category**	**Intention**	**Desired Outcome**
Priority 1	God	Bible Study	Grow in relation-
		Prayer	ship with Christ.
		Worship	Better reflect him
		Listen	and his love.

Priority 1

_____

_____

Priority 2

_____

_____

Priority 3

_____

_____

Priority 4

_____

_____

Priority 5

_____

_____

Review your list of priorities. Anything misaligned? Is your top priority in line with God's wisdom? Hint: read the scripture below.

> But seek first his kingdom and his righteousness,
> and all these things will be given to you as well.

> —Matthew 6:33 (NIV)

If so, continue to draw near to God and take special note of how *he* is leading you to be intentional about living this priority and his desired outcome—his glory and your good. If not, seriously consider whether or not you are willing to surrender to God's will in this area of your life and what change would be required for you to do so.

When you're clear about your purpose and your priorities,
you can painlessly discard whatever does not support these, whether
it's clutter in your cabinets or commitments on your calendar.

—Victoria Moran

Priorities and Roles Bring Clarity

Your list of God-inspired priorities is related to your values *and* intricately tied to your roles. When you determine your priorities, you more easily recognize what roles and activities are meant to fill the hours of your day.

An ongoing review and acknowledgement of your priorities helps bring clarity to the authentic you, your purpose, and how you go about living it. This is important because your God-determined HeartSong is deeply connected to the God-given hours of your days.

Priorities that Distract

Amy Carmichael served as a missionary in Japan beginning in the 1890s. She tells the story of going to an elderly, dying woman to share the gospel, wearing her very English clothing including her beautiful fur-lined gloves. The woman was listening intently to what Amy shared about Jesus until she was distracted from the message by Amy's gloves. This was a light bulb moment for Amy. Suddenly, she realized that in her desire to spend her very precious time and money on shopping, purchasing, and wearing such clothing (a priority for her), she might cost the eternal life of others. She never again wore more than the native and simple kimono while in Japan.[1]

We may never be called to mission work in a foreign country, but this story makes me wonder if there are misplaced priorities in our lives that might open the door for distraction from Christ and the message we are called to share.

How might you be spending precious time and money on priorities that keep you from sharing your message? In what ways might this be distracting or keeping others from Christ?

_____

_____

_____

When we put God first, all other things fall into their proper place or drop out of our lives. Our love of the Lord will govern the claims for our affection, the demands on our time, the interests we pursue, and the order of our priorities.

—Ezra Taft Benson

Your God-determined
HeartSong is deeply connected
to the God-given hours
of your days.

HEART CHALLENGE 3

Your Roles and Life Balance

There is no role too challenging
for you when you hold the hand of God.
God has proven to be faithful since the beginning of time.
And, God gives good advice about saying no to opportunities
that could prevent you from completing
the work God gave you to do.[2]

—Carla Barnhill

I confess. I've had a life-long struggle with FOMO. Apparently, this is a fairly common phenomenon in our busy world. Have you heard of it? *FOMO* is an acronym for *fear of missing out*.

Oxford Dictionaries define FOMO as "anxiety that an exciting or interesting event may currently be happening elsewhere."

For me, the crux of the problem with FOMO has been making a right decision. It's not so much about missing out on an activity or event as it is about missing out on choosing the best, right thing. There are really great roles that lead to wonderful activities that I'd like to say yes to, but only about seventeen waking hours in my day.

Knowing our HeartSong helps us choose the right roles and spend our time wisely. But here's the deal…and for me this was an ah-ha moment: To know your HeartSong you must believe in your heart your identity is in Christ (you are who God says you are) rather than believing who you are is tied to your roles. This belief brings with it the freedom to accept the parts he's called you to play and decline others. You aren't meant to be and do everything for everybody—which leads to struggle, overwhelm, and burnout. You are called to be and do some things for others by God's design, strength, and power. With this in mind, Heart Challenge three begins by identifying your current roles and asking and answering this question:

How do I choose between good and God-appointed roles when they all seem to be calling my name?

I spend a tremendous amount of time carefully choosing the roles I wish to play so that I can run from the role I was born to play. And if I keep on doing that, I will eventually set foot in my grave never having set foot on the stage.

—Craig D. Lounsbrough

Identifying Your Current Roles

Our roles are many in this world. Some of mine include wife, mom, daughter, sister, writer, life coach, entrepreneur, friend…and the list goes on. What are your current roles? What roles do you believe you were you born to play? This next exercise helps you define them and the amount of time you dedicate to each.

- Write down your current life roles. As many as you can.

- Check the ones you believe are God-ordained roles and place a question mark after the ones you're not absolutely clear fit your design.

- Now, estimate how much time you contribute to each life role every day, week, or month.

	Role	Time Contribution: Day/Week/Month
1.		
2.		
3.		
4.		
5.		
6.		
7.		
8.		

Ask yourself: *Are my roles and time spent on them consistent with my priorities?* (Step Two, Heart Challenge 2) Anything pop out at you? Explain.

_____

_____

_____

Balance and Boundaries

I have to ask, if you struggle with balance, have you considered the boundaries you have or haven't set on your time, activities, and life? God is the creator of boundaries. He begins his story with them.

Consider Adam and Eve and the border God set for them: "You may freely eat the fruit of every tree in the garden—except the tree of the knowledge of good and evil. If you eat its fruit, you are sure to die." (Genesis 2:16–17) Think about the limit Jesus set on his time after he heard Lazarus was sick. We're told, "So although Jesus loved Martha, Mary, and Lazarus, he stayed where he was for the next two days." Why? "…For now you will really believe." (John 11:5–6,15)

Boundaries. God creates them with intention and purpose because he loves us and wants the best for us. Boundaries make space for more of him and the life we're meant to live.

What boundaries have you or will you set so you can pace your days and your life according to God's direction? Look back on your roles and time spent on each. What needs to change? Name at least one boundary you are willing to set today to create more space in your life.

———————————————————————————————

———————————————————————————————

———————————————————————————————

> The woman of Proverbs 31 is not just a busy woman.
> She is a woman who knows her purpose in God.
>
> —Dr. Myles Munroe

Walking and Working in Rhythm with God

In a world where we're desperate for balance in our days, we wonder if it's even possible. For me, finding and staying balanced in life conjures up an image of walking a tight rope high above ground, working with all my might to find the perfect mark before falling to one side or the other. Just thinking about the delicacy of making this happen is rather stressful. Do you know what I mean? While feeling and living out-of-balance isn't our preference, the fact is, Jesus doesn't tell us to live balanced lives. He *does* teach and command us to follow him and his example. We've just learned one way to imitate Jesus is to set boundaries. And if we examine his ways more closely, we also see he walks and works in rhythm with God.

Creating Rhythm

In scripture, we see Jesus pushed on toward his destiny every day, getting away to be alone with God frequently. "But Jesus often withdrew to the wilderness for prayer" (Luke 5:16). Scripture also tells us once Jesus was so tired he slept in a boat during a fierce storm. "Jesus was sleeping at the back of the boat with his head on a cushion." (Mark 4:38) Now, that's tired!

Sleep and rest is clearly important to God and to our health, but sometimes, and in some seasons, we simply don't get enough of it. Amidst those periods, we need to intentionally create time to withdraw to be alone with God for restoration. Jesus set the example. We are to follow him.

We don't read of Jesus running here and there concerned about his time. He set out each day attending to all God placed before him, knowing to whom and what he was called. As Jesus headed toward fulfillment of his destiny, he stopped with ease and intention to serve others all along the way. Within his service, he created space—a type of rhythm and rest as he pursued his purpose.

Perhaps it was his focus on his relationship with God and doing his Father's will that kept Jesus from stressing about a lack of time—for if anyone had a sense of the end nearing and time running out, it had to have been Christ.

What would it mean to you to intentionally shift your attention toward God and his good, abundant, and perfect will for you in each day's tasks, interruptions, and looming deadlines?

_____

_____

_____

Rather than thinking in terms of finding this elusive thing called life balance, will you consider your time with the idea of creating an ease or rhythm to your days and within your God-inspired boundaries?

Like Jesus, your rhythm will surely begin by cultivating your relationship with the Lord. Are you willing to make time alone with him happen? And what about your focus during your day? Some people find it helpful to set reminders on their phones or devices to step away from their work to rest and pray. Just a few minutes alone with God can help you refocus, refresh, and allow him to lead the way.

What are you willing to do to intentionally create time to rest and be alone with God? How will you focus on him and what he wants to accomplish through you each day?

_____

_____

_____

While you evaluate your roles, rest, and rhythm, here's another point to ponder: In the end, maybe what you *really* seek is not so much balance but a calming of the storm in your soul. What if what your heart needs, even more than balance, is peace? Of course, your body requires sleep and your mind needs rest.

But, where will you find your peace?

Come to me. Get away with me and you'll recover your life.
I'll show you how to take a real rest. Walk with me and work with
me—watch how I do it. Learn the unforced rhythms of grace.
I won't lay anything heavy or ill-fitting on you.
Keep company with me and you'll learn to live freely and lightly.

—Matthew 11:28 (MSG)

The Gift of Peace

If we look at the world through our humanness rather than with a heavenly perspective, there is a case to be made for a lack of peace—otherwise known as anxiety. In his knowing all the troubles and sadness we would experience in our lives, Jesus tells us in John 14:27: "I am leaving you with a gift—peace of mind and heart. And the peace I give is a gift the world cannot give. So don't be troubled or afraid." In Philippians 4:6-7 Paul instructs us: "Do not be anxious about anything, but in every situation, by prayer and petition, with thanksgiving, present your requests to God. And the peace of God, which transcends all understanding, will guard your hearts and your minds."

What does all this mean for you?

1. You were given and received a 'gift' when you repented and accepted Christ as your Savior. This gift comes in a package called the Holy Spirit—the Spirit of Christ (Acts 2:38).

2. You can experience peace of mind and heart. You don't have to be anxious or afraid because you have the Holy Spirit and he is your Helper forever (John 14:16).

3. When you feel anxious, pray instead of worry. Thank God for his peace that surpasses all understanding (Philippians 4:7). You can trust he will protect your heart and your mind.

There are many questions and answers the world provides as to the worry we experience but I wonder, would our anxiety lessen if we believed Jesus and were transformed by his truth? And what if we determine to be more mindful to apply Paul's instructions each time anxiety attempts to keep us stuck and blinded to God's loving protection and goodness? What if you and I actually sought to conquer our anxiety the moment it hits by turning to Jesus in prayer?

Do you believe you can and are meant to experience peace through the power and gift of God's Holy Spirit? Take a moment and name any current anxiety you are experiencing and write a prayer thanking God for the Holy Spirit and his gift of peace within your heart and mind just as Christ promised.

_____

_____

_____

I have told you this so that you may have peace in me.
Here on earth you will have many trials and sorrows.
But take heart, because I have overcome the world.

—John 16:33

In the end,
maybe what you really seek
is not so much balance but a calming
of the storm in your soul.

HEART CHALLENGE 4

Your MindSet

Then a little blue engine came down the track, and she was asked to pull the cars… "I'm not very big," said the Little Blue Engine. "They use me only for switching in the yard. I have never been over the mountain."… Then she said, "I think I can." And she hitched herself to the little train… Puff, puff, chug, chug, went the little blue engine. "I think I can—I think I can—I think I can—I think I can— I think I can—I think I can—I think I can—I think I can."

—The Little Blue Engine, *The Little Engine That Could*

The Little Engine That Could is a story of optimism and hard work. We like to share it with our children. And if we dig deep enough, we see it is more than that. It's a tale about mindset.

Your Mindset Is Your Life

Mindset might be defined as a philosophy of life, a system of beliefs or attitudes that affect your choices and behaviors. Your mind and what it's set on largely define the life you lead. Not only does research play this out but God, no less, tells us so.

86

And you must love the Lord your God with all your heart,
all your soul, with all your mind, and all your strength.

—Mark 12:30

Set your mind on things above, not on earthly things.

—Colossians 3:2 (NIV)

For as he thinks within himself, so he is.

—Proverbs 23:7 (NAS)

Clearly, your mindset is important and directly related to fulfilling your God-designed purpose and living your HeartSong.

Discovering Your Mindset

Carol Dweck, Ph.D., author of *Mindset: The New Psychology of Success*, identifies two ways people view themselves.

- *Fixed Mindset:* "Believing that your qualities are carved in stone," creating an "urgency to prove yourself over and over." Failure is personal and an end point. You feel judged and supersensitive to mistakes. Everything is good news or bad news.[3]
- *Growth Mindset:* Believing that "your basic qualities can be cultivated through your efforts." Your life situation at any given time is a starting point for development. You are oriented toward learning and converting setbacks into future successes. Perseverance leads to creative achievement.[4]

Which mindset do you agree with most? A fixed or growth mindset?

_____

_____

_____

What scripture reference(s) can you find that best reflect and support the mindset you've just agreed with?

_____

_____

_____

Does knowing you are of sacred worth and the love you have for yourself (no ego here) play a role in your mindset? Please explain.

_____

_____

_____

Why do you think your mindset matters to God? To your life?

_____

_____

_____

What specific changes in your mindset, if any, would you be willing to make to more consistently align with the mind of Christ? What is your first step to making this change?

_____

_____

_____

For we have the mind of Christ.

—1 Corinthians 2:16

More on Mindset

Set your mind on things above.

—Colossians 3:2 (NIV)

Abundance Versus Scarcity Mindset

One morning, during my time of prayer and devotion, I prayed to God this prayer.

> *I seek to have the mind of Christ that I may know*
> *your will.*
> *I seek to have the willing obedience of Christ that I*
> *may do it.*
> *I seek to have the passion of Christ that I may have*
> *the perseverance to complete it!*

A word of caution…be careful what you pray for.

The very next morning, the Holy Spirit spoke these words to my heart.

> *Stop living in lack! My yoke is not heavy.*
> *You live in the land of plenty—*
> *I will take care of you.*
> *Be patient. Wait.*
> *Do my will.*

If you'll notice, my first request of God was to have the mind of Christ. God's first response to me was, "Stop living in lack!" Then, he went on to teach me:

If you want the mind of Christ, the first thing you need to do is accept that you already have it. You aren't lacking in this. Then, you need to make room for and use it. Stop thinking about what you don't have. Live instead with thanks for your abundant life. You've got plenty of all that you need!

It was a heart-piercing and humbling revelation. God was calling me to live in the present, by his Spirit, and change my mindset from one of scarcity to one of abundance.

Gratitude builds a bridge to abundance.

—Roy Bennett

Benefits of an Abundant Mindset

The importance of an abundance mindset is mentioned throughout the Old and New Testaments as God tells us over and over again to praise and give thanks.

Enter his gates with thanksgiving; go into his courts with praise. Give thanks to him and praise his name.

—Psalm 100:4

Has no one returned to give glory to God except this foreigner?

—Luke 17:18

Always be joyful. Never stop praying. Be
thankful in all circumstances, for this is God's
will for you who belong to Christ Jesus.

—1 Thessalonians 5:16–18

The call to be grateful and give thanks for the abundance of our lives is not commanded in order to satisfy a needy God, although he surely enjoys and is glorified by it. *The call to be grateful for the abundance in which you and I live is for our benefit and the benefit of others.*

How does this last statement apply to your life? What might be the benefits?

_____

_____

_____

What are you thankful for today? Will you choose to think on those things? Will you choose to thank and praise God for them?

_____

_____

_____

In her best-selling book, *One Thousand Gifts*, Ann Voskamp writes as a woman who "discovered, in giving thanks for the life she already had, she found the life she'd always wanted."[5]

How might this quote be relative to your life?

_____

_____

_____

The Focus of Your Mindset

Every day and in all things God desires we open his gifts of breath, relationships, and circumstances—our abundant lives—with a grateful heart.

But, instead, we often focus on what we find missing as Satan whispers to us and our flesh agrees to our cravings for attention, approval, awards, self-satisfaction, and the list goes on.

How do we know if we are living with a scarcity or abundance mindset?

A scarcity mindset focuses on what is missing…lacking. It is to suffer through our limited resources and resent when others ask for more.

A mindset of abundance focuses attention on the fullness of what we've been given and what good God has in store for us—no matter our circumstances, that we might be generous to others.

A scarcity mindset is a focus on self. At its depth, it is driven by pride and applauded by evil. It keeps us living small and within ourselves.

An abundance mindset is focused on Christ and others. It is driven by love and grateful acceptance of God's provision. Angels most assuredly applaud an abundance mindset as it brings growth to self, to those around us, and to his Kingdom.

If you lean toward a scarcity mindset or live it full on, why would it be worth it to you to make an intentional change to a mindset of abundance?

_____

_____

_____

> The thief comes only to steal and kill and destroy; I have come that they may have life, and that they may have it abundantly.

> —John 10:10 (NAS)

Living in Abundance

If you are reading this, abundant living has been made available to you whether you've chosen to accept it or not.

An abundant life is what Jesus came to give. But to enjoy it, you may have to do what I've had to learn to do. Intentionally refocus your thoughts and give thanks!

Write a prayer of praise to God below thanking him for the abundance of your life today and for your future.

_____

_____

_____

What action steps can you take to remain and grow in gratefulness to God through Christ Jesus for all he has done for you?

_____

_____

_____

How might an abundance mindset change your life? The lives of others? Your relationship with God?

_____

_____

_____

What scripture(s) might help you remember to refocus your mindset as you go about your day?

_____

_____

_____

The abundance mentality springs from internal security,
not from external rankings, comparisons, opinions, or associations.

—Stephen R. Covey

One Last Thing…

We know God offers freely an abundant provision of grace (Romans 5:17). But we might not remember he also tells us in Proverbs 28:19 (NIV), "He who works his land will have abundant food—but the one who chooses fantasies will have his fill of poverty."

While our first thoughts should include thanksgiving and gratefulness for the richness of God's unending grace, we have a role to play in creating abundance as well. We have a responsibility to do what he has given us to do in our days. We're not meant to sit around and simply dream or wish for abundance. Nor are we to keep it to ourselves. We are to share our plenty with others. There is work to be done that leads to our abundance and God's glory.

When you think of the work God has given you to do today, do you think of it with a grateful heart? Do you think of your work in the light of abundance? Or do you think of your work in terms of what is lacking?

_____

_____

_____

What practical ways will you make an abundance mindset come alive in your days regarding your work?

_____

_____

_____

In what ways is your heart stirred to share your abundance with others?

_____

_____

_____

The abundant life is not a measure of life at all, but a way of living.
It is not about having but about giving.

—Luis G. Padraja

Your mind and
what it's set on
largely define
the life you lead.

HEART CHALLENGE 5

Conquering Your Thought Life

Watch your thoughts; they become words.
Watch your words; they become actions.
Watch your actions; they become habits.
Watch your habits; they become character.
Watch your character; it becomes your destiny.

—Lao Tzu

You've learned your mindset is a set of beliefs—your philosophy of life. What you must also know is your thoughts, emotions, attitudes, and actions are all intertwined. And, they are either aligned with God's will or they are allowed to lead you astray and away from God's purposes. What's a believer to do? You must be intentional. You must pay attention to what you are paying attention to! Fulfilling your inspired dream and purpose requires you to examine the thoughts that are allowed to drift through and hang out in your mind…the thoughts you dwell upon.

Your thoughts have power. They have a voice—remarkably like your own. And unless you harness them, they will tell you lies to keep you bound, trapped, and defeated.

So, I have to ask. What are you thinking?

Don't copy the behavior and customs of the world, but let God transform you into a new person by changing the way you think. Then you will know God's will for you, which is good and pleasing and perfect.

—Romans 12:2

Conquering your thought life is one of the most important things you can do to overcome obstacles to knowing and living your HeartSong. With this knowledge, it's time to do some *mindful* research.

Take a minimum of forty-eight hours and write down…

- Your negative, condescending, or accusatory thoughts. Example: *I'm stupid. I can't. I won't ever be able to…. They'll think I'm crazy. They'll laugh at me. I look fat. I'm ugly. I'm too young. I'm too old. I'll never be happy again.*
- Your prideful thoughts. In some cases, we might think too highly of ourselves. Thoughts like: *I'm better than she is. I'll do it my way. No need to work at it, I'm a natural. I don't need them they need me. I'm the boss, I have all the answers.* Such thinking entangles us in self. Ultimately, these thoughts ensure alienation and defeat.

Listen closely for two days. Record your negative, dishonoring, prideful, and untrue thoughts over the next forty-eight hours.

_____

_____

_____

Any surprises about what you discovered? Do you see the enemy at work in the thoughts you've written? Are you ready to fight for truth in your life—to ditch any wrong, accusatory, limiting, and prideful thinking? If so, get ready to step into the victory Jesus won long ago on your behalf!

Change your thoughts and you change your world.

—Norman Vincent Peale

Breaking Free from Your Thought Chains

There is a well-known story about elephants, ropes, and chains. Maybe you've heard it.

If a rope is put around a baby elephant's back leg, the rope is hooked to a stake driven into the ground, and the baby elephant is restrained there until he can take care of himself. Once freed, the elephant will not venture away beyond the length of the rope that had once kept him in place.

The elephant has been conditioned to accept his mental prison.

We aren't elephants but our thoughts can keep us tied to lies. Chained. Stuck. If we let them, they slip their way around our lives and we believe we must remain imprisoned. Our mental chains keep us frozen in place. But, unlike elephants, we can remove our ropes and chains by intentionally changing our thoughts.

You are braver than you believe,
stronger than you seem, and smarter than you think.

—Christopher Robin, *Winnie-the-Pooh*

Science Supports Scripture

In her book, *Switch On Your Brain*, Dr. Caroline Leaf records what her scientific research revealed: *As we consciously direct our thinking, we can wire out toxic patterns of thinking and replace them with healthy thoughts.*[6]

In other words, Dr. Leaf's research supports God's call to be intentional about what you think. You are meant to *think on purpose*!

Your life is shaped by your thoughts.

—Proverbs 4:23 (GNT)

Dr. Leaf explains the God-designed science behind all this. "When you bring a thought into consciousness, you also bring up the attached emotion. When the thought along with its emotions bubble up into the conscious mind, you *feel* the emotions."

She goes on to teach that a thought plus its attached emotions creates a state of mind called an attitude. Your attitude "influences what you say and do." Changing your thoughts changes your emotions and feelings which affect your attitudes. These changes then determine your words, actions, and outcomes. Can you see how changing your thoughts will change your life?

The question we all should ask and answer as we go through the moments of our days—the question we *must* ask and answer if we want to live our most fulfilling, successful, and God-honoring lives—is this:

What thoughts am I allowing myself to think?

Good and true thoughts lead to good and true attitudes and actions. The opposite is also correct.

The Battle for Your Thought Life

> For though we live in the world, we do not wage war as the
> world does. The weapons we fight with are not the weapons
> of the world. On the contrary, they have divine power to
> demolish strongholds. We demolish arguments and every
> pretension that sets itself up against the knowledge of God, and
> we take captive every thought to make it obedient to Christ.
>
> —2 Corinthians 10:3–5

Life is a battle. I doubt you disagree. Part of the battle (it could be argued—most of the battle) includes fighting against wrong, pretentious, and destructive thinking. Like any warrior who experiences victory, you must do your part. You must take your life-diminishing thoughts captive. How?

1. *Intentionally pay attention.* Make it a habit to listen for and write your factually and spiritually untrue, debilitating, fear-and anger-inducing thinking (like you did previously) so you can take those thoughts captive to Christ. Literally, offer them up, hand them over to Christ, and repent. Then, ask the Holy Spirit to make it extra-apparent when your thoughts are not God-honoring and true. And most importantly, ask him to reveal the lie you believe because of these thoughts.

   To do this requires being deliberate and attentive to the thoughts entering your mind. In my life, inherited traits, life experiences, and self-indulgent practices plus the taunting whispers of the enemy can make it easy to think and get stuck on a lie that leads to a heart-felt belief, resulting in a life-diminishing action. Make no mistake; this untrue belief wants more than anything to suck the life out of me rather than allow me to think on and believe God's loving truth within me. Over time, I've learned, by God's grace and the Holy Spirit's leading, to more quickly notice the lie that would keep me living small and feeling trapped. Now, I'm intent on taking each thought captive to Christ as he lovingly exchanges them for the truth my heart yearns to believe.

Thinking and believing a lie will only serve to deceive and destroy and you will be left living a less-than life. Instead, why not root out and expose the lie and let the light of the Holy Spirit transform it *and* you?

2. *Put on your armor. Specifically, the helmet of Salvation.* Ephesians chapter six teaches us that to fulfill our duty in the battles of life on Earth, we are to put on the "belt of truth and the body armor of God's righteousness. For shoes, put on the peace that comes from the Good News. In addition, hold up the shield of faith." And then this: "Put on salvation as your helmet."

So what's the deal about the helmet? Well, what's the purpose of a helmet? I can hear you saying it now. *To protect my head.* Right! What's in your head? *My brain.* Correct again! What happens in your brain? *I think!* Understanding that there are lots of incredible things going on in our brains, this scripture speaks directly to protecting your mind—your thoughts. And get this; the word salvation references defense and deliverance from harm. The word helmet? In the Greek it means the seizing or encirclement of the head. And head? The part most readily seized.

The enemy will attack whatever is most easily seized. Your head—your thoughts. He will do it subtly, swiftly, and often. He knows where we are most vulnerable.

But in his eagerness to destroy us, he forgets about our forever-loving God and Father who has revealed to us the helmet of salvation by way of the crown of thorns encircling Jesus's head. What a humbling and sweet reminder— it is Jesus Christ we are to put on. He is our covering. He is our defense and deliverance from harm. He is our helmet of salvation.

3. *Take the sword of the Spirit, which is the word of God.* Defeat the destructive thoughts and lies with God's word. Ephesians 6:17 reveals his word—the sword—is our only offensive weapon within God's armor. We're to exchange the lies we're tempted to believe for his truth. Do you know the truth, God's word? His good and righteous words of truth are what we're meant to think.

Replacing life-destroying lies with God's word renews our minds and aligns us with God's will and the power of Christ. This, the victorious power of Jesus, is the living, conquering authority of scripture.

Jesus himself teaches, "I am the way and the truth and the life." And, "If you hold to my teaching…then you will know the truth, and the truth will set you free" (John 14:6; John 8:32). Jesus is truth, and his teaching embodies the truth. Truth can't be changed no matter what anyone else thinks or says, or does. Truth defeats wrong thinking, lies, and beliefs every time because of Jesus's defeat of Satan once and for all long ago. It's history. And as we know, we can't change the past. We can only pretend it doesn't exist.

You and me? We need to move past the thought we can do it all out of pure, self-propelled will. Our part is to choose to listen, believe the truth, put on our helmet, and wield our weapon. We need to actively exchange our disparaging thoughts to hope-filled ones inspired by heaven and made possible by the cross. We may need to ask for help and that's okay. We aren't meant to do life alone. Once we begin cutting away the lies and God's loving truth is allowed to fill the space, we will experience the freedom already within us whispering, waiting to be heard and believed:

You are good enough. You can overcome. You have purpose.

Applying God's Mind-Changing Instructions

> Don't copy the behavior and customs of this world,
> but let God transform you into a new person
> by changing the way you think.
>
> —Romans 12:2

It's time to wield your weapon—the truth. The sword of the Spirit. Christ himself. The word of God.

To apply this mind-changing thinking in a practical way: *

- Write down the life–debilitating thinking you previously recorded on page 98.

---

* *These steps are adapted from Dr. Caroline Leaf's scientifically researched "21-Day Brain Detox Plan." Her detailed plan can be found in her book, Switch on Your Brain.*

- Find words, phrases, verses, and even lyrics to hymns and songs that speak scriptural truth to your heart and directly apply to your life.
- Write down and speak aloud your selected words of truth next to your defeating thoughts. Record what Jesus speaks to your heart as you *focus on the truth.*
- Pray and meditate about these praiseworthy and excellent truths and how they are better than the negative for your life and the lives of others.
- Reveal the truth by your action. Take a step to act on the truth Jesus has shared with you. Write your action step below.

_____

_____

_____

_____

_____

_____

_____

We are only freed by the truth—not what we believe to be the truth.

—Tony Evans

Never let fear, procrastination or the longing
for approval from others take possession of your mind;
they become self-forged chains.

—Ty Howard

A Word About Feelings

Our feelings are real. Remember, they're attached to our emotions. God designed us this way. Ever wonder why? I have. As someone who really feels her feelings, I know how easy it is to let them lead my life. But God's will is always for his glory and our good by way of the Holy Spirit's guidance. Our emotions and feelings are meant to bring fullness of life. However, they need Holy Spirit-driven direction.

Since coming to understand thoughts have attached emotions that I *feel*, I know if I follow the Holy Spirit's prompting and change my thinking, God's transforming power changes the emotion and the feeling attached to it. Sometimes we let ourselves dwell on and wallow in self-pity or self-righteous anger or weirdly enough, even sadness. But it's not where we're meant to stay. My feelings aren't to be denied or ignored. Neither are yours. Feelings are God's idea. Jesus showed and shared his feelings. They make him relatable, like they do us. Feelings have purpose. Ultimately, they are signposts. Signals meant to turn us toward and draw us closer to God.

Recognizing Feelings as Turn Signals

> His purpose was for the nations to seek after God and
> perhaps feel their way toward him and find him—
> though he is not far from any one of us.
>
> —Acts 17:27

In Greek, the word, "feel," here means to *verify by contact, to touch, to search for*. Could it be feelings really do act as signals directing us to seek and turn toward our loving God? When we feel happy—he calls us to rejoice with him. When we feel sad or discouraged—he calls us to draw near to be comforted and directed by him. When we feel angry—he calls us…you get the idea!

What a great way to stay in constant communion with our Lord! He invites us to turn to him and share every wonderful, frustrating, joy-filled, and painful moment with him. Because through Christ, he identifies with our feelings. All of them.

Yet (and this is worth reading aloud), throughout his mission, Jesus never allowed his feelings to override his purpose. Jesus felt human feelings and then he directed them. He wants that for us, too. And so he invites us to come—feel our way toward him and find him—for comfort, direction, understanding, and love so we can *know him* and continue *with him* on the path to our purpose.

No matter your feelings, remember, God is signaling you to turn to him. To draw near. Turning requires an open and humble mind. You have to do your part. But when you do, you'll see, like the Israelites, if you let yourself *feel* your way toward God, you will find him.

What emotions are you feeling today? Right now? Will you turn toward God and share your heart with him?

_____

_____

_____

What does he want you to know?

_____

_____

_____

He taught me I had to live by my faith and not by my emotions.
He showed me that I must learn to trust Him, to have confidence
in His unfailing love and devotion, regardless of how I felt.

—Samuel Logan Brengle

We need to actively
exchange our disparaging
thoughts to hope-filled ones inspired by
heaven and made possible by the cross.

HEART CHALLENGE 6

Christ-Like Character Traits

> God intended for us to carry our strengths,
> our weaknesses, our personality, our character
> into every circumstance.
>
> —Priscilla Schirer

Your character greatly influences the tenor of your HeartSong.

Each day you are given the opportunity to respond to people and circumstances with Christ-like character. As you choose to apply godly traits to your days, you move closer to singing your song as it's meant to be sung.

Below, and following, you'll find nine Christ-like character traits. There are more, but this list is quite common to our day-to-day living.

As you read through this list, you'll notice many of these traits overlap with God's definition of *love*.

Contentment	Patience	Confidence
Perseverance	Humility	Courage
Self-Control	Love	Truth

Because you are made to reflect the character of Christ, it's good to examine how much of him you are letting shine through. No worries. This exercise isn't meant to discourage you, but to encourage you to move closer to Christ and allow his character to become ever more evident as you move through your days—your life.

- Under each Christ-like character trait and its definition, mark the number on the scale of one to ten that best indicates the level at which the trait is reflected in your life today. One indicates an ongoing struggle to respond this way. Ten indicates you regularly respond this way in your daily living.[7]*

Contentment

Not that I was ever in need, for I have learned how to be content with whatever I have. Philippians 4:11
Definition: Sufficiency.

|--|
  1   2   3   4   5   6   7   8   9   10

Patience

Be patient with each other, making allowances for each other's faults because of your love. Ephesians 4:2 (NIV)
Definition: To bear. Long-suffering. Endure.

|--|
  1   2   3   4   5   6   7   8   9   10

---

* Definitions come from James Strong, *Strong's Exhaustive Concordance of the Bible* (Nashville, TN: Thomas Nelson, 1990).

Confidence

Such confidence we have through Christ before God. 2 Corinthians 3:4 (NIV)
Definition: Sure. Believe. Trust.

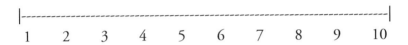

Perseverance

Let perseverance finish its work so that you may be mature and complete, not lacking anything. James 1:4 (NIV)
Definition: Persistency.

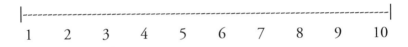

Humility

Do nothing out of selfish ambition or vain conceit. Rather, in humility value others above yourselves. Philippians 2:3 (NIV)
Definition: Bring low.

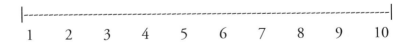

Courage

So be strong and courageous! Do not be afraid and do not panic before them for the Lord your God will personally go ahead of you. He will neither fail nor abandon you. Deuteronomy 31:6
Definition: Make strong. Prevail.

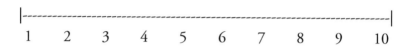

|--|
1   2   3   4   5   6   7   8   9   10

Self-Control

A person without self-control is like a city with broken-down walls. Proverbs 25:28
Definition: Mastery. Sound mind.

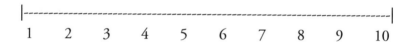

|--|
1   2   3   4   5   6   7   8   9   10

Truth

Only fear the Lord and serve Him in truth with all your heart; for consider what great things He has done for you. 1 Samuel 12:24
Definition: Right. Sure.

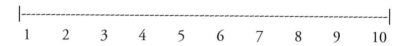

|--|
1   2   3   4   5   6   7   8   9   10

Love

> *Ever since I first heard of your strong faith in the Lord Jesus and your love for God's people everywhere, I have not stopped thanking God for you. Ephesians 1:15–16*
> *Definition: Affection. Benevolence.*

|---|
| 1   2   3   4   5   6   7   8   9   10

What Christ-like character traits resonated most with your Spirit when you read about them?

_____

_____

_____

Which do you struggle to reveal most? Why do you think this might be?

_____

_____

_____

Is there a thought and belief relative to your areas of struggle that God desires to change and that will allow Christ's character to live freely through you? What is he saying to your heart right now?

_____

_____

_____

So, no matter what I say, what I believe, and what I do,
I'm bankrupt without love.

—1 Corinthians 13:3–7 (MSG)

Because you are made
to reflect the character of Christ,
it's good to examine how much of
him you are letting shine through.

HEART CHALLENGE 7

Identifying Your
Character Strengths

Strength does not come from winning.
Your struggles develop your strengths.
When you go through hardships
and decide not to surrender,
that is strength.

—Mahatma Gandhi

Heart Challenge seven helps you get specific about your character strengths.

Why are your character strengths so important? Living with Christ-like character (Step 2, Heart Challenge 6) and leaning into your predominant strengths allows you to be true to the you God created. And they help point you toward your HeartSong.

Evaluating your strengths also reveals areas where you're not as strong. (I know—ugh.) But it's not all bad. God often uses these areas to reveal *his* strength. Remember what he told Paul in 2 Corinthians 12:9 after Paul asked three times for the thorn in his flesh to be removed? "My grace is all you need. My power works best in weakness."

God's point in calling you to your HeartSong is to love on you, strengthen you, transform you, and work through you so you can and will share with others the grace he has shown you as you do your part to the fulfillment of his Master Plan.

God calls you along your special path. And as you walk with Christ, you get to choose to be strengthened by him and share his love and grace poured out for you—or not.

> Being like Jesus means loving.
> It also means hard, painful obedience.
> Christ leads us on a path of struggle toward the death of our wills and our personal plans.
> Our every dream is subdued to his will. This is where God is glorified and others are served.
>
> —Author Unknown

The VIA Institute On Character offers a free personality assessment and your next step is to take it. This personal survey recognizes twenty-four character strengths. The results are ranked according to prevalence; those ranked higher are most likely to be representative of you and those strengths ranked lower tend to come less naturally. The resulting insight provides you with an opportunity to intentionally live into your strengths and seek Christ's help in the lesser of the categories.

Character Strengths Revealed

I'll go first for the big assessment reveal. My number one character strength, according to the VIA assessment, is perseverance. I feel good about this as it affirms my diligence. My husband will tell you without a doubt, I like to finish what I start. It's just in me.

Perseverance has been an important attribute in my personal, professional, and spiritual life. It has benefited me, those around me, and God's Kingdom.

On the other end of the spectrum my lesser strength, again according to this survey, is self-regulation. The Bible calls it *self-control*. Unfortunately, when I thought about it, I had to agree. Being disciplined about my appetites and splurges is something I continue to work on with God. For the truth is, self-control for the believer is really *God-control*. Self-control, like other character strengths is based on inviting in, listening to, believing and obeying the Holy Spirit throughout the day so his power within you is worked out and displayed to others. Not for your glory, for his.

Like my higher-ranked strengths, my lesser ones impact God's kingdom and those around me. Satan, our enemy, has no qualms about using my lower strengths to induce discouragement, confusion, and defeat. He will do whatever it takes to keep you and me from living our inspired dream and God-designed purpose. But Satan forgets, as we turn to God he works through us transforming love, strength, and peace. What a gracious reminder of his sufficient and glorious presence.

> Last of all I want to remind you, your strength must come from the Lord's mighty power within you.
>
> —Ephesians 6:10 (TLB)

Assessing Your Strengths

It's your turn to discover what this assessment reveals about your character strengths.

- Go to the website below to locate and complete the *Free Via Character Strengths Test.*[8]
- Download or print the results of your assessment so you may refer to them as desired.

Free Via Character Strengths Survey Link
www.viacharacter.org

Take a moment to reflect and comment on your strengths and their ranking. Then write down additional thoughts you have about specific and intentional ways you might best share your strengths and strengthen your lesser character traits as you live your day-to-day life in love and honor to God.

_____

_____

_____

_____

_____

_____

_____

For I can do everything through Christ
who gives me strength.

—Philippians 4:13

God's point in calling you
to your HeartSong is to love on you,
strengthen you, transform you,
and work through you…

HEART CHALLENGE 8

What Is Your Motive?

The Lord searches every heart and understands
every motive behind the thoughts.

—1 Chronicles 28:9 (NIV)

Motives. They are the reasons behind the things you do—the choices you make.

Whether you realize it or not, there is a motive behind everything you do. Your motive may be pure, good, and right or your motive may be impure, manipulative, and wrong. Either way, you get to choose your motives.

The thing is, to make good and right choices and live your most meaningful life, you have to pay attention to your motives. You and I often don't recognize our wrong motives until we stop, dig a little deeper, and begin to ask the question: *Why am I doing this...really?*

In order to make forward progress, keep from stumbling or getting stuck and rehashing life experiences (God's re-test of our motives?), we have to answer the *why* question honestly.

Why Am I Doing This?

Motives may include such things as fear, money, attention, approval, responsibility, boredom, unrighteous anger, envy, and pride. Impure motives. Or, motives may be pure and established in love.

As I've grown in my faith, I've often been led to question my motives. I'll admit, there have been many times my *why* has not been pure but instead based in pride, jealousy, anger, and fear.

I've heard myself saying, "*I don't want to spend my time _____*" (fill in the blank). Why? Because I'm afraid *I* won't get done what *I* planned to do. Which also, by the way, clearly reveals my motives: pride and greed. *Ouch!*

I often forget my time is not my own. But, I must surrender my time, along with everything else to God. Saying no to something because I want to horde my time is not a pure motive. There are good and valid reasons to say no. Being greedy with my time is not one of them.

What I observe most about my wrong motives is that they are, *uh-hum*, all about me. In Rick Warren's book, *The Purpose Driven Life,* he boldly reminds us in just four words to get our motives in line with God's:

It's not about you.[9]

This is a rather earth-shattering revelation if one isn't prepared to read it—like I wasn't. Nevertheless, the shock value didn't make it any less true for me. Our lives are not about us *and* our lives are not our own.

Our lives are about Christ and we belong to the One who created us.

The Better Motive

Jesus tells us his motive is twofold; obedience to God and his desire that we, his followers live with delight beyond measure.

> For I have come down from heaven to do the will
> of God who sent me, not to do my own will.
>
> —John 6:38

> I have come so they may have and enjoy
> life, and have it in abundance.
>
> —John 10:10 (AMP)

Jesus's motive wasn't himself, his needs, and human preferences here on earth. Jesus was motivated by love. Love of God and love for you and me.

> It's motive alone that gives character
> to the actions of men.
>
> —Jean de la Bruyère

Examining Your Motives

The following scriptures reveal the importance God places on our motives.

> *But I, the Lord, search all hearts and examine secret motives.*
>
> *—Jeremiah 17:10*

WHAT IS YOUR MOTIVE?

God brings our darkest secrets to light and reveals our private motives.

—1 Corinthians 4:5

*And even when you ask, you don't get it because your motives
are all wrong—you only want what will give you pleasure.*

—James 4:3

Here are three lessons I take away from these scriptures. See if
you agree.

1. The Lord thinks our motives are important enough to
   search and examine them.
2. Eventually, our true motives will be revealed. The truth is,
   God already knows and sees the why of what we seek and
   so might others.
3. Motivations of self-promotion and pleasure indicate
   self-sufficiency and pride. They block God's yes response
   to our prayers. Why not, like David in Psalm 26:2, ask
   God to test your motives and your heart? Such a request is
   a sign of loyalty, trust, and surrender to his will.

Stop now and ask yourself the why of your wants and desires.
Are the experiences, outcomes or possessions you seek based on God-
honoring and selfless motives? Thoughtfully and honestly consider
the motive for your current longings and prayers.

Your Want or Desired Action   Your Motive for It

_____   _____

_____   _____

_____   _____

How do you think God views your motives? What changes, if any, do you need to make?

_____

_____

_____

Choosing Pure Motives Means Struggle and Surrender

Whether your motive for doing something is hording your time, envy, fear, gaining attention, selfish pride, or lust, once you've named and claimed a wrong motive, the struggle begins. It's your will against God's. *(The old life against the new life. See Ephesians 4:21-24.)*

When I think about Jesus and his understanding of our motives, I remember when he entered the Garden of Gethsemane to pray. It's clear, before being arrested, tried, and ultimately sent to the cross, Jesus struggled with the thought of enduring the path before him.

> *Abba, Father…everything is possible for you. Please take this cup of suffering away from me.*
>
> —*Mark 14:36*

For a time, the human part of Jesus was *overwhelmed with sorrow* (Mark 14:34, NIV)—as anyone would be. Perhaps he even sought another road to our salvation. Why? I believe the human motive behind the struggle had to have been fear. Fear of the pain of crucifixion, fear of separation from God while bearing our sin, or maybe fear for us and our pain or unbelief.

But, after spending time with God in prayer, Jesus's motivation changed. His fear was overcome by God's love.

Yet not as I will, but as you will.

—Mark 14:36 (NIV)

It's the same for you and me. The only pure motive is this: God-glorifying *love.* Action motivated by love calls for continual surrender of our will to God's. Any other motive does not bear fruit (love, joy, peace, patience, kindness, goodness, faithfulness, gentleness, and self-control. Galatians 5:22) because it isn't connected to God through Christ. When we surrender out of obligation, legalism or false humility, good things can happen, but they don't bear Kingdom fruit. Only as we surrender our impure motives with a humble heart, accept God's forgiveness and grace in Christ, and share this limitless grace with others as God has purposed do we begin to experience the new life we deep down really crave.

Your God-Revealed Motives

What decision do you need to make about doing this or that—this job over that one, this way of spending your time over that one, and so on? Rather than reacting immediately, getting advice from friends, or making a list of pros and cons, why not ask, *does my motive glorify God?* Then, do what Jesus did. Pour out your heart to God. He'll reveal your motivations, and if need be, guide you to realign them.

When you ask, you do not receive, because
you ask with wrong motives,
that you may spend what you get on your pleasures…
Submit yourselves, then, to God.

—James 4:3,7 (NIV)

The only pure motive is this:
God-glorifying *love*.

HEART CHALLENGE 9

Overcoming Fear

The only calibration that counts is how much heart people invest,
how much they ignore their fears of being
hurt or caught out or humiliated.
And the only thing people regret is that
they didn't live boldly enough,
that they didn't invest enough heart, didn't love enough.
Nothing else really counts at all.

—Ted Hughes

Take a moment and think about what words you would use to describe fear. Did *melted mess* come to mind?

Melt is the word used often in the Old Testament to describe fear. It means to dissolve, to utterly discourage.

At this the hearts of the people melted
in fear and became like water.

—Joshua 7:5 (NIV)

I'm not sure about you, but I know my heart has melted more than once. And, I have been utterly discouraged. Opportunities for growth and happiness have disappeared as my heart dissolved into a watery pool due to fear...fear of pain, loss, humiliation, defeat, responsibility, sorrow for another or myself. Can you relate?

Here's another thing. Have you noticed fear grows the more you pay attention to it? I hate to say it, but fear easily snatches and traps us in its jaws when we open the door and allow our *focus on and faith in our fear* to become greater than our *focus on and faith in God's love.*

> Such love has no fear,
> because perfect love expels all fear.
>
> —1 John 4:18

Why Are You Afraid?

> For God has not given us the spirit of fear and timidity,
> but of power, love, and self-discipline.
>
> —2 Timothy 1:7

To overcome fear, we must first identify it. Our fear(s) may be long-standing or come upon us in the moment. Either way, we are told throughout scripture, we are not to be afraid.

What is Fear?

In the verse above, fear is defined in the Greek as *dread*—a word noticeably similar to *dead*. *Strong's Exhaustive Concordance* reports by implication, fear is faithlessness. Could it be that fear is the death of faith?

Understanding fear in this light, it's not surprising that fear (dread and faithlessness) is one of the enemy's favorite tools for manipulating us. Can you think of anything that would discourage us, make us more miserable, cause us to live smaller, more diminished lives than destroying us with fear and killing our dreams? Satan uses fear to keep us exactly where he wants us: stuck and unable or unwilling to accept the life God has already prepared for us.

Not surprisingly, he does this by whispering fear-inducing thoughts. Here's an example.

Satan doesn't want me writing, coaching, or teaching those who need encouragement and guidance. He would most assuredly prefer I stay bound by fear. In the past, it wasn't uncommon for me to hear thoughts such as, *Who am I to share this message? What can I possibly tell them that they want and need to hear or don't already know? They'll reject what I say. What difference will I really make any way?*

What fears do those words portray? Fear of rejection, not being good enough—deep-seated fears from past life experiences. Fears that hope to stay hidden. But fears that must be named and brought before the power and light of Christ. Because there, its roots become exposed and die. Little by little or all at once. Whatever God allows for your good and his glory.

As we learned previously, we get to choose what we think. So, while my fears may seem valid at the time, I *always* get to choose to change my fearful thoughts to *faith-filled* ones. I also get to choose to hold on to and hide my fear or by faith, let go and expose it. This faith does not believe *I* am the overcomer. This faith believes Christ is the one—having already demolished the spirit of fear and filled me with his Spirit.

When I remember and believe this, I really *can* do what he has given me to do because *he* is doing it through me. This is true for you, too! You can be who you are meant to be and do what the Lord has called you to do. You don't have to accept and be bound by the spirit of fear. You don't have to be afraid!

What's Your Fear Experience?

Have you ever been asked to use your gifts and talents to serve but were too afraid to say yes?

_____

_____

_____

What might have gone missing because *you* were missing?

_____

_____

_____

What fear may have been, or perhaps still is, holding you back?

_____

_____

_____

Do you remember the source of this fear? The first time you felt it? Record your thoughts.

_____

_____

_____

What scripture(s) can you find to shine light on this fear to help you let it go and expose it?

_____

_____

_____

Do you see how, in reality, you have a role to play in conquering fear? Do you see that if you permit it, fear can hold you back from what God has called you to be and do? If so, the next question must be: *How do you conquer your fear and build your faith?*

So faith comes by hearing, and hearing by the word of Christ.

—Romans 10: 17

Remember the story of Peter walking on the water toward Jesus (Matthew 14:28–32)? Peter, full of faith, slipped over the side of the boat *onto* the rough water. He knew there were risks involved, but he believed Jesus, stepped forward, and literally walked on water. Until…he changed his focus. Scripture says, "But when he saw the strong wind and the waves he was terrified and began to sink" (v. 30).

It wasn't that Peter didn't already know it was too windy and wavy to attempt this walk. We're told previously his disciples were fighting a "strong wind" and "heavy waves." Yet, Peter's excitement and faith in Jesus spurred him to go overboard.

Now, let's take a look at John 1:1 which says this, "In the beginning was the Word, and the Word was with God, and the Word was God." And in Revelation 19:13, we learn, *He wore a robe dipped in blood, and his title was the Word of God.* The Word that John speaks of in the Books of John and Revelation is Jesus. Jesus is the embodiment and fulfillment of God's Word. Where are we to look and who are we to believe when we're afraid? Jesus… God's Word. The one offensive weapon (we learned previously but it's worth repeating) God has given us with which to fight.

Initially, Peter wasn't looking at the storm. He believed and was focused on Jesus. It was when he changed his focus that his faith faltered. He became afraid. And, what did Jesus say? *You have so little faith, why did you doubt me (Matthew 14:31)?* Peter became faith-less because as he looked away he became fear-full.

Do not be afraid, for I am with you.

—Isaiah 41:10

Satan has every desire to keep you from your most fulfilling life. He wants you focusing on your circumstances and on your fear. Not on Jesus. Not on his *Word*.

Feeling Fear

Whenever you *feel* fear (remember, feelings are a signal to draw near to God), take a moment to ask:

1. What exactly is my fear?
2. What experience(s), thoughts, and beliefs are influencing my fear?
3. Where is my focus?
4. What truth does God's Word teach about my fear?
5. Who and what am I choosing to believe?

Take your time and list below any fear(s) you currently harbor. Ask yourself the questions above relative to each specific fear. What action step will you take today toward overcoming one or more of your fears?

_____

_____

_____

_____

_____

Because of Love

1 John 4:8 tells us *God is love.* Later, this passage reveals as believers in Christ, *love (God) is made complete among us so we will have confidence.* You and I can be assured in our faith because of love *(God).* And because love *(God)* expels all fear (1 John 4:18).

When fear strikes, where do you focus? Your circumstances? Self? Most of us do.

I'm sure you've realized you cannot get through this life without experiencing fear. It slithers in.

But God says, *I am with you. I am love. I am your confidence. I am more powerful than your fear. I Am.*

Will you believe him? Will you trust him? Will you draw near? Will you let Love overcome your fear?

What would Love overcoming fear look like in your life?

_____

_____

_____

Fear's Purpose

Often, as we desire to step into knowing and living our inspired dream and God-designed purpose, fear rears its ugly head. Which begs the question, "Why would God allow fear to take hold of me if all I really want to do is answer his call on my life?"

Why do you think God would allow fear to creep into your heart and your life?

_____

_____

_____

Don't feel shy or intimidated by the experience.
You may face some unexpected criticism,
but be prepared for it with confidence.

—Jack Canfield

Confidence and Courage Over Fear

God doesn't tell us we should or can overcome fear on our own. But he does teach us that when we trust in him, we don't have to be afraid. We can meet what's been set before us with confidence and courage because of his love and power working within us. If we define *confidence* as faith that we can do something in spite of its difficulty and *courage* as the willingness to do something in spite of fear, then our part is to 1) believe and trust in God whose empowering love conquers fear, and 2) act on this belief.

The following women of the Bible exemplify confidence and courage by their actions. What other traits do they display as they live out their unique calling?

Mary: (Luke 1)_____

Esther: (Esther 4)_____

Abigail: (1 Samuel 25)_____

Rahab: (Joshua 2)_____

Describe a situation where you relied on God for confidence and courage and acted in spite of your fear. What other traits did you display as you moved through the experience?

_____

_____

_____

Are you willing to take a risk, surrender your fears, and walk boldly in faith *(And keep on doing it!)* to fulfill God's calling—your purpose?

_____

_____

_____

Action steps are listed on the following page to help you exhibit confidence and courage as you lean into God and toward your HeartSong. Pick at least one of the steps and make it your focus this week.

Or, create your own action step(s).

Confident and Courageous Action

- Intentionally take a risk. Try something you're afraid to attempt.
- Admit when you are wrong; be yourself; tell the truth.
- Defend your godly beliefs. In humility and confidence, stand up for yourself. Stand up for God.
- Fight against injustice with loving action—not words alone.
- Reach out. Speak to someone you don't know.
- Get out of your comfort zone. Assist someone who needs help.

My Confident and Courageous Actions Steps for the Week

1.
2.
3.

"What do you fear, lady?" [Aragorn] asked.
"A cage," [Éowyn] said.
"To stay behind bars, until use and old age accept them,
and all chance of doing great deeds is gone beyond recall or desire."

—J.R.R. Tolkien, *The Return of the King*

You don't have to accept
and be bound by the spirit of fear.
You don't have to be afraid!

HEART CHALLENGE 10

Your Grief Matters

Grief is the price we pay for love.

—Queen Elizabeth II

Grief. It's the deepest, darkest, sharpest, and yet dullest pain of all. It is sadness, loneliness, and even fear squeezing together in the depths of our souls.

Grief comes in many ways: loss of life, rejection, divorce, illness, bankruptcy, natural disasters, joblessness, brutality, humiliation, and more. Dr. Diane Langberg, a renowned trauma expert, writes in her book, *Suffering and the Heart of God,* "Grief is the result of some kind of death." And adds, "Death is not something we only encounter at the end of our lives, is it? We meet it hundreds of times in a lifetime. We meet it in every ending."[10]

Grief's response may be pain, fear, anger, and sorrow. Your grief may involve a personal experience or your grief may be on behalf of another's loss or choices. Or both. When grief's time comes, the enemy's desire is to drag us deep into darkness. Attempting to bind us. Hopeless.

But God

My most life-affecting grief at this writing has come with divorce. The loss and despair were daggers that cut deep. I thought I'd never recover. I felt lost and alone. I felt rejected and afraid. Helpless and hopeless. I could hardly breathe or believe it was really happening. But, there it was. My dream shattered—my marriage dead—right before my eyes.

But God slowly drew me to him. I devoured scripture and gained strength. It really was *a light for my path* (Psalm 119:105). A light that gave me a *future and a hope* (Jerimiah 29:11), somehow richer and more tender because of my grief.

This grief hasn't left me, but has transformed me. It's forever a part of my becoming who God intends me to be. My experience of grief was meant by the enemy to destroy, *but God,* just as he promised, has used my pain for good in so many ways. Maybe not always good as we like to feel and think of it right here and right now, but a deeper and forever good. A good we see only when we let ourselves look at the sorrows of life from a heavenly perspective, knowing nothing but ultimate goodness results from our God who is nothing but good.

You are called to a *but God* experience, too. The darkest side of grief will try to steal the life you're meant to live. But, it can't stop God from using the experience as a shining light for you and others as you believe and turn toward him.

All praise to God, the Father of our Lord Jesus Christ.
God is our merciful Father and the source of all comfort.
He comforts us in all our troubles so that we can comfort others.
When they are troubled, we will be able to give them
the same comfort God has given us.

—2 Corinthians 1:3–4

The Companion Called Grief

Grief is a companion of the heart. Even though it comes uninvited, it must be allowed to do its work. In the midst of your loss, grief appears as your enemy, but once it arrives, it is meant to stir within you and become your tender friend. Grief begins as gut-wrenching pain, and if allowed, becomes the gentle reminder this isn't our home after all. Slowly, if you allow the Spirit to do his transforming work, the sadness turns to compassion, and the grief that has kept us imprisoned invites us to pass its care and comfort to another.

Your grief may result from death of many sorts. *But God* will surely use it to add the tenderness, grace, and love needed to live your unique and important HeartSong boldly and sweetly so others may, too.

> For everything there is a season, a time for every
> activity under heaven. A time to cry and a time to
> laugh. A time to mourn and a time to dance.
>
> —Ecclesiastes 3:1,4

Pause for a moment. Close your eyes. Take a deep breath. Now, list every grief experience you remember having and the ones you are currently going through.[11]

_____

_____

_____

This can be a difficult. Thank you for your honesty and vulnerability.

Do you find you still have open wounds where grief dwells?

_____

_____

_____

Do you believe your grief matters to God? Why or why not?

_____

_____

_____

What do you think God is saying to you at this moment about any grief you may be experiencing or have experienced?

_____

_____

_____

How do you sense God might want you to apply your grief experience(s) to your HeartSong?

_____

_____

_____

Grief does not change you...
It reveals you.

—John Green, *The Fault in Our Stars*

Grief begins as gut-wrenching pain,
and if allowed,
becomes the gentle reminder
this isn't our home after all.

Heart
Challenge 11

Forgiving and Living

To forgive is to set a prisoner free and discover
that the prisoner was you.

—Lewis B. Smedes

Un-forgiveness is often found on many a believer's HeartSong journey. Oh, it's usually hiding, but if you truly want to move forward and live your most meaningful, meant-to-be, God-honoring life, it cannot be fully experienced with un-forgiveness lurking in the shadows.

Someone once said, *Un-forgiveness is like drinking poison yourself and hoping the other person dies.*

The bitterness of un-forgiveness brings with it bondage, anger, revenge, and quite often the loss of a dream.

Forgiveness is the opposite. Forgiveness brings life and healing. Forgiveness cleanses. It lightens your burdens and opens the way for love and transformation.

Below is a link to a video that offers insight into forgiveness. This is recorded testimony of Corrie Ten Boom, survivor of the Nazi Holocaust, entitled *How to Forgive*.[12]

I pray this story stirs in you a yearning to allow Christ to move through you to forgive any and every life-diminishing anger, hurt, or hate that has kept you from letting go, forgiving, loving, and living your inspired dream and purpose.

Be sure to type the title or link into your browser correctly!
https://www.youtube.com/watch?v=3cfp51vLZb4

Reflect on any un-forgiveness you may harbor. Use the following space to write and clarify your thoughts. Will you choose to forgive?

_____

_____

_____

If you choose not to forgive, what might be holding you back?

_____

_____

_____

How might you justify any un-forgiveness in light of God's love and forgiveness toward you?

_____

_____

_____

And forgive us our sins, as we forgive those who sin against us.

—*Matthew 6:12*

145

Forgive Yourself and Be Forgiven

When we speak of the need to forgive, we're usually talking about forgiving someone else. However, there are times when we need to forgive ourselves or seek forgiveness from others.

Paul tells us in Acts 10:43, "Everyone who believes in him will have their sins forgiven through his name."

God through Isaiah says, "I am the God who forgives your sins, and I do this because of who I am. I will not hold your sins against you" (Isaiah 43:25, GNT).

Jesus commands in Matthew 5:23 (NIV), "Therefore, if you are offering your gift at the altar and there remember that your brother has something against you, leave your gift there in front of the altar. First go and be reconciled to your brother; then come and offer your gift."

And in Romans 8:1—just in case you don't remember, this might help *you* forgive *you*: *So now there is no condemnation for those who belong to Christ Jesus.*

Do you harbor any un-forgiveness toward yourself? Use the following space to write and clarify your thoughts. Will you choose to forgive yourself?

_____

_____

_____

Will you seek forgiveness and allow yourself to be forgiven by others?

_____

_____

_____

Reflect on Matthew 5:23. If this applies to you today, what step(s) will you take to make this happen?

_____

_____

_____

What difference do you think forgiveness might make to living your HeartSong?

_____

_____

_____

> I think that if God forgives us we must forgive ourselves.
> Otherwise, it is almost like setting up ourselves
> as a higher tribunal than Him.
>
> —C.S. Lewis

Forgiveness brings life and healing.
Forgiveness cleanses.
It lightens your burdens and opens
the way for love and transformation.

HEART CHALLENGE 12

Habits and Attitudes

We are what we repeatedly do.
Excellence, then, is not an act but a habit.

—Aristotle

We all have them. Habits, that is.

Some are good, weird, bad, destructive, constructive, healthy, or unhealthy. We develop habits over time, and they slowly but steadily move us forward, backward, or keep us stuck.

Identifying our good and constructive habits, as well as our bad and destructive ones, helps us break free and move closer to living our most God-honoring and fulfilling lives.

So, let's name them! Make a list of your good and bad habits. The word "good" here encompasses constructive and healthy habits. The word "bad" includes destructive and unhealthy habits. Next to each habit, write your motive for it.

No powder puff, kinda-sorta, it's not really that-big-of-a-deal answers here. Be brutally honest and transparent with yourself.

List habits you have developed that are good and give you forward momentum.
Good habits (Include spiritual habits.)

_____

_____

_____

List habits you have developed that are destructive and keep you stuck or push you backward and further from experiencing God's best for your life.

Bad habits (This is the brutally honest and transparent part.)

_____

_____

_____

Now, go back and write down your motivation for your good and bad habits. Dig deep. What's the perceived or real pay-off?

Here's an example. Let's say I have a bad habit of gossiping. What's my motivation? Deep down, I want to appear in the know, maybe better or smarter than the person I'm talking about to gain recognition and approval. Maybe I'm angry with her and want to ruin her other friendships, so I can get even and she can feel as badly as I do. Then, I think I can gain a greater sense of significance.

See what I mean by perceived pay-off? I think by participating in this habit it will be good for me but in reality the pay-off is broken relationships of all sorts—including my relationship with Christ.

Let's home in here. What word might God use for this thing we're prone to do rather than the words *bad habits*? Does *sin* come to mind? Granted, there are bad habits that aren't sin—let's say cracking your knuckles or tapping your foot incessantly. Those things are more of an annoyance. Unless your motive is sinful...to drive others crazy! But, we're talking about the bad habits that keep us broken and out of relationship with God. He calls them sin.

Try this. Close your eyes. Name your bad habit(s) and visualize surrendering them to Jesus. Hand them to him as you stand together at the foot of the cross. Talk to Jesus, what do you say? Then, Jesus, looking you in the eyes, speaks to you. What does he say to you?

_____

_____

_____

Why do you think giving up your bad habits is important to Christ? To living your HeartSong?

_____

_____

_____

Read Romans 8:1–14. How do you think this scripture passage might relate to turning away from bad habits?

_____

_____

_____

What would (or does) it feel like to be led by the Spirit and turn away from what Paul says in Romans 8:12 "your sinful nature urges you to do?"

_____

_____

_____

The next time you are tempted to fall into a bad habit, listen to the Spirit prompting you to turn away toward truth. Recall Jesus's words to you as you pray and surrender to Christ's love.

Nothing so needs reforming
as other people's bad habits.

—Mark Twain

What's Your Attitude?

Your attitude should be the same as that of Christ Jesus:
Who being in very nature God, did not consider equality with God
something to be grasped, but made himself nothing, taking
the very nature of a servant, being made in human likeness.
And being found in appearance as a man, he humbled himself
and became obedient to death—even death on a cross!

—Philippians 2:5–8 (NIV)

After reading this scripture, it sure seems like having the same attitude as Christ is a pretty tall order. Breaking down Paul's words to the Philippians may help. Reread the verses above. See if you discover in verse eight the dominant attitudes revealed in Christ's action.

Do you see the attitudes he displayed? *Humility and obedience.*

Charles Swindoll, a Christian pastor, author, educator, and radio preacher has this to say about attitude.

The longer I live, the more I realize the impact of attitude on life. Attitude, to me, is more important than facts. It is more important than the past, than education, than money, than circumstances, than failures, than successes, than what other people think or say or do. It is more important than appearance, giftedness, or skill. It will make or break a company...a church...a home. The remarkable thing is we have a choice every day regarding the attitude we will embrace for that day. We cannot change the inevitable. The only thing we can do is play on the one string we have, and that is our attitude.... I am convinced that life is 10% what happens to me, and 90% how I react to it. And so it is with you...we are in charge of our attitudes.[13]

It's nice to know there is something we can actually control. The question is, do we? Remembering our attitudes are directly linked to our thoughts and emotions, what is the best way for you to control your attitude?

_____

_____

_____

Maybe my spunky ninety-nine-year-old Aunt Elaine will inspire your thinking (and therefore your attitude) like she did mine. Once, when visiting with her, I noticed she smiled and laughed even as she struggled to hear, participate in conversation, and move along with her walker. As we hugged goodbye, I commented on how she always seemed to have a great attitude. Her response? *Why not?* I love her answer, don't you? *Why not*, indeed!

> But understand that with an attitude like that,
> there'll be no glory in it for you.
>
> —Judges 4:9 (MSG)

153

Humility

The word humility in the Greek is defined as lowliness of mind, esteeming one another, empty conceit. To put the word even further into focus, it would be correct to say the opposite of humility is pride.

There are lots of attitudes we can have: positive, good, bad, mean-spirited, prideful, humble, etc. Take this opportunity to check in with yourself and ask:

What's my current attitude?

_____

_____

_____

Who or what do I have a bad attitude about/toward?
(Nothing and no one can be your answer if it's true.)

_____

_____

_____

How do you think your thoughts and mindset affect your attitude?

_____

_____

_____

What is God calling you to do so you can live with an attitude of humility?

_____

_____

_____

Will you choose an attitude of humility?

_____

_____

_____

Why or why not?

_____

_____

_____

True humility is not thinking less of yourself;
it's thinking of yourself less.

—C.S. Lewis

Obedience

I never thought of obedience as an attitude until pondering the Philippians 2:5–8 scripture. And I never thought of my attitude equating to my lifestyle until reading this:

Obeying God sometimes seems like the hardest road to take.
But in the long run, it is the only lifestyle that
brings real peace and genuine joy.

—Unknown

The Greek definition of the word "obedience" is to submit, absolutely.

Knowing this, ask yourself:

Are there areas of my life in which I have not absolutely submitted to God? If yes, they include the following:

_____

_____

_____

Who or what is keeping me from obeying God in this area?

_____

_____

_____

How might my thoughts play a role in my attitude of disobedience?

_____

_____

_____

What is God calling me to do today to be obedient?

_____

_____

_____

Will you choose an attitude of obedience? If yes, how does your choice affect your day-to-day living? Your future?

_____

_____

_____

> Does it make sense to pray for guidance about the future
> if we are not obeying in the thing that lies before us today?
>
> —Elisabeth Elliot

Our attitudes are directly linked
to our thoughts and emotions.

STEP THREE

Casting Your Dream.
Claiming Your Purpose.
Taking Action.

Moving Forward as God Leads

Welcome to the final step of your journey! So far, you have completed what can be a challenging and difficult trail. Introspection and character-building is often not easy. And if we were to walk this road without the arms and cloak of Christ wrapped around us, it is a trip to transformation we would likely not take on—or put on, as the apostle Paul describes it. But as believers, we choose the change because of Jesus's love.

Only a few more challenges remain to prepare and inform you about your HeartSong. First, as a reminder, let's review the entire premise—the stepping stones—of this journey you've been traveling.

- God is your Father.
- God created, chose, and loves you. You belong to him.
- God says you are worthy.
- God designed you in a unique way for a reason. He wants you to be you.
- God wrote a song on your heart before you were born. He gave you a dream.
- God has called you to a more-important-than-you-can-imagine purpose.
- God invites you to draw near to him, to overcome what holds you back, and to live in his strength and character.
- God knows the joy and fulfillment you'll experience as you live your HeartSong, share it with others, and bring glory to his name.

Notice how all of this is about God and his ideas. Not you and yours. Not me and mine. And, because we have a loving Father and he has an unending and utterly unfathomable love for us, we don't have to do life on our own. Out of his love, grace, and mercy God helps us along our way by pouring into each of us the Holy Spirit of Christ. Who by the way, doesn't come empty handed, he comes bearing gifts!

HEART CHALLENGE 1

Discerning Your Spiritual Gifts

You have inside you the capacity to invest your mental, emotional,
and spiritual gifts in a way that glorifies God,
impacts the world, and satisfies
your soul.

—David Jeremiah

God knows we cannot live our HeartSong apart from him. And
so, he desires we choose to respond out of love and in humble obedience to the guidance and prompting of the Holy Spirit.

It is no longer I who live, but Christ lives in me.

—Galatians 2:20

Part of what the Holy Spirit does in a believer's life is to give
each of us spiritual gifts. These gifts help propel and accomplish our
purpose as we use and share them with others to glorify God and
build up his Church.

> A spiritual gift is given to each of us so we can help each other. It is the one and only Spirit who distributes all these gifts. He alone decides which gift each person should have.
>
> —1 Corinthians 12:7, 11

Do you know your spiritual gifts? Are you using and sharing them with others? This is foundational to your success and fulfillment. For when you invite the Holy Spirit in and are attuned to him in the moments of your day—using your spiritual gifts as he directs—you live your best life. *And* you experience joy and peace because it's God working in and through you (1 Corinthians 12:6).

Spiritual Gifts Bring Glory to God

I love to sing. I feel God's pleasure when I do.

I realize I'll never be a recording artist. Nor do I have the best voice in the choir. Singing isn't a spiritual gift. It's part talent and part skill. Something inherent in me and something developed. Singing helps me fulfill my purpose, as it is a way for me to express and put to use one of my *spiritual gifts* and help build up the church: the gift of exhortation.

Exhortation means to encourage, to call upon and help strengthen believers, to guide them to truth. It is my primary spiritual gift. Singing is just one way I am able to use my gift of encouragement to draw others near to God.

Music is in my family's blood and in mine. God designed us this way. God also determined my distinct purpose. Once I accepted Christ as my Savior, the Holy Spirit deposited in me the gift of encouragement to help accomplish this purpose. I am meant to use music as one way to encourage others and draw them closer to Christ. Beyond singing for the parson, as my husband would put it, biblical life coaching allows me to use my spiritual gift of encouragement to help strengthen believers, to guide them to truth, draw near to Christ, and fulfill their destiny. This creates joy in their lives (and mine), affects others for Christ, helps strengthen the body, and glorifies God. Knowing and using your spiritual gifts helps you do the same.

> When you do most what you do best,
> you put a smile on God's face.
> What could be better than that?
>
> —Max Lucado

What God Says About Spiritual Gifts

> In his grace, God has given us different gifts for doing
> certain things well. So if God has given you the ability to
> prophesy, speak out with as much faith as God has given
> you. If your gift is serving others, serve them well. If you are
> a teacher, teach well. If your gift is to encourage others, be
> encouraging. If it is giving, give generously. If God has given
> you leadership ability, take the responsibility seriously. And if
> you have a gift for showing kindness to others, do it gladly.
>
> —Romans 12:6–8

A spiritual gift is given to each of us so we can help each other. To one person the Spirit gives the ability to give wise advice; to another the same Spirit gives a message of special knowledge. The same Spirit gives great faith to another, and to someone else the one Spirit gives the gift of healing. He gives one person the power to perform miracles, and another the ability to prophesy. He gives someone else the ability to discern whether a message is from the Spirit of God or from another spirit. Still another person is given the ability to speak in unknown languages, while another is given the ability to interpret what is being said. It is the one and only Spirit who distributes all these gifts. He alone decides which gift each person should have.

—1 Corinthians 12:7–11

It was he who gave some to be apostles, some to be prophets, some to be evangelists, and some to be pastors and teachers, to prepare God's people for works of service so that the body of Christ may be built up until we all reach unity in the faith and in the knowledge of the Son of God and become mature, attaining to the whole measure of the fullness of Christ.

—Ephesians 4:11–13(NIV)

God has given each of you a gift from his great variety of spiritual gifts. Use them well to serve one another.

—1 Peter 4:10

Do not neglect the spiritual gift you received.

—1 Timothy 4:14

It's clear from these scriptures:

- As believers, we have received spiritual gifts.
- The Holy Spirit has determined and given us our gifts.
- Using our gifts helps prepare others for works of service.

- Our works of service help build up the body of Christ and unite us in faith.
- We should not neglect our gifts.

Discerning Your Spiritual Gifts

Jeff Jernigan, Ph.D., LPC, and coach offers the following information about our spiritual gifts.

1. When using our gifts, our work and ministry seem effortless—it is even energizing.
2. When we operate outside our giftedness, we encounter friction and fatigue.
3. There is a difference between gifts and talents/skills/abilities.
   - Talents, skills, and abilities may be innate or learned.
   - Gifts can be refined with training and experience, but they are not innate or learned. They are gifts from the Holy Spirit.
   - Under enough pressure, our talents/skills/abilities disappear, and only the gifts continue to operate.
4. Spiritual gifts develop as a function of age and experience.
   - As our primary gift emerges and grows, related gifts appear and become stronger in their support of our primary gift.
   - Gifts become the lens through which other aspects of our design find expression.
   - We are called to express all the gifts. For example, we are called to be merciful even if we do not have the gift of mercy.[1]

Do you know your spiritual gifts? This is your opportunity to gain insight in this area. Take this spiritual gifts inventory online at **www.spiritualgiftstest.com** and look forward to what you are about to discover.[2]

Do you agree with your results? Any surprises? Ask those who know you well if they see these gifts in you or if they've experienced you using them. Next, consider how God wants you to use your spiritual gifts to build up his church. Pray about it. Then brainstorm at least three ideas with your coach, partner or group.

1.
2.
3.

How might your spiritual gifts play a role in living your HeartSong?

_____

_____

_____

The bird does not sing because it has the answer.
It sings because it has a song.

—Chinese Proverb

For when you invite the Holy Spirit in
and are attuned to him in the
moments of your day—using
your spiritual gifts as he directs—
you live your best life.

HEART CHALLENGE 2

Be Inspired

Today, you inspired me.

—Unknown

Seeking and walking out your dreams and purpose are what you are meant to do. But nobody said it would be easy. Knowing this, our good God offers his divinely breathed touches of joy amidst our journey in simple and meaningful ways meant to delight, encourage, and inspire us as we go along. If you're hard-pressed to find inspiration, asking a few reflective questions may help.

What inspires and fuels you to keep going? What are the thoughts, things, beliefs, people, and places that rekindle your spirit, attitude, and strength? What calls you to be creative, innovative, or imaginative?

Identifying what inspires you is significant. Spontaneous or planned inspiration helps you refresh, reset, and reinvigorate as you navigate the road set before you.

Your inspiration may be God's word, music, nature, a friend, an article, a family member, a hobby, a book, a painting, a movie, or a prayer. God can use many things that suit you—and his purposes—to surprise you, fill you up, and keep you on track.

Inspiration isn't escape from something or someone to another place. Inspiration is what causes you to go on, refuel, learn, grow, and create. Inspiration? It's a gift—a gift that helps you enjoy and complete your journey.

The whole Bible was given to us by inspiration from God.

—2 Timothy 3

What Inspires You?

There are many things that inspire me: a cardinal's song, color, and presence; scripture; witnessing loving kindness; a Sunday afternoon nap on my hammock; a friend's encouragement; a weekend away; my husband and kids; music. And more.

Take a moment and write below what and who inspires you most. Be as specific as you can.

_____

_____

_____

_____

_____

_____

_____

When was the last time you noticed or did any of these things? When was the last time you talked or spent time with any of these people?

_____

_____

_____

Do you need to take a trip down inspiration lane? How and when will you do this?

_____

_____

_____

Share your ideas with your coach, partner, or group. Discuss why you think your inspirations might be important to you and your HeartSong.

We remember before our God and Father
your work produced by faith,
your labor prompted by love, and your endurance
inspired by hope in our Lord Jesus Christ.

—1 Thessalonians 1:3 (NIV)

Inspiration?
It's a gift—a gift
that helps you enjoy and
complete your journey.

HEART CHALLENGE 3

Remembering Your Success

And the Lord replied,
"I myself will go with you and give you success."

—Exodus 33:14 (TLB)

What are your successes? We've all had them. Small successes, large ones, quiet ones, public ones. Success that brings trophies, ribbons, and hugs. Success that resounds not with human applause but an ovation of angels.

When you look back on your life, do you first notice the hard times, the regrets? Is what you see filled with moments, days, or perhaps years of struggle, and I would've, could've, should've? If so, it's time to remember your successes.

Why? Like trials, your successes have a role to play in God's purpose for your life.

But before we move on, let's define the word *success*.

How do you define success?

_____

_____

How does God defines success? What biblical reference(s) can you find to support this definition?

_____

_____

_____

Does your definition of success differ from how God defines it? If so, how? Why might this matter?

_____

_____

_____

Successes Accomplish His Purposes—and Yours

While Paul reminds us in Philippians chapter four to *forget what is behind,* God reveals his desire for our success, and his hand in it, to be remembered.

The following exercise is meant to help you gain additional understanding of how remembering your successes can make a godly difference in your life and the lives of others.

1. Look up the following scriptures.
2. Read the entire passage to get a clear understanding.
3. Describe the resulting success of each situation.
4. Write down the feelings, emotions, behaviors you suppose the situation invoked at the time. Ex: joy, humility, boldness, love, obedience, etc.
5. How did the outcome of each experience impact and bring success to future generations?

Exodus 12:1–14. *This day shall be a day of remembrance for you.* (v.14, NRSV)

*Resulting Success:*_____

*Feelings, Emotions, Behaviors:*_____

*Success of Future Generations:*_____

Matthew 26:1–13. *I tell you the truth, wherever the Good News is preached throughout the world, this woman's deed will be remembered and discussed.* (v. 13, NLT)

*Resulting Success:*_____

*Feelings, Emotions, Behaviors:*_____

*Success of Future Generations:*_____

Luke 22:14–19. *Then he took a loaf of bread, and when he had given thanks, he broke it and gave it to them, saying, "This is my body, which is given for you. Do this in remembrance of me."* (v. 19, NRSVA)

*Resulting Success:*_____

*Feelings, Emotions, Behaviors:*_____

*Success of Future Generations:*_____

Do you see how your successes may go unnoticed by the world? Do you understand how remembering the successes God grants impact your life and the lives of others? Your HeartSong? Explain.

_____

_____

_____

Success in God's eyes is faithfulness to His calling.

—Billy Graham

Remembering Your Success

Think about the successes in your life. Don't be shy. There's no room for false humility here. Include anything the Holy Spirit brings to mind the world may not see as success but Jesus does.

Defining your successes is an important piece to moving forward. Use the following timelines to identify and write down your life successes. Be sure to include as many as you can remember, no matter how large, small, silent, or acclaimed.

Example

Childhood (0–12)

    Learned to ride bike   Won poetry and drawing contest

|------------------|----------------------------------|------------------|

Your Successes

Childhood (0–12)

|---|

|---|

Teen Years (13–19)

|--|

|--|

Young Adult (20–35)

|--|

|--|

Middle Aged (36–51)

|--|

|--|

Maturity (52 →)

|--|

|--|

As you review your successful experiences, name the feelings and behaviors they stirred up at the time.

_____

_____

_____

What feelings and behaviors does remembering your successes invoke now?

_____

_____

_____

Looking back, do you see God's hand in these experiences? What might he have been teaching you?

_____

_____

_____

How might your successes have affected others then—and how might they affect others now?

_____

_____

_____

How might remembering your successes help impact and direct your daily actions?

_____

_____

_____

Do your past successes shed any light on your future path?
If so, how?

_____

_____

_____

You must remember your successes.
Not to the extent that you walk in pride, but so you
acknowledge God's grace, power, and love works through you.
For His desire to express His love leads to the
desires of your heart.

—G. L. & S.H.

Like trials,
your successes
have a role to play
in God's purpose for your life.

HEART CHALLENGE 4

Your Passions

> Passion is the fuel that gives successful people
> the energy needed to keep pursuing their dreams.
>
> —John Maxwell

The Latin root of the word *passion* is *pati*. It means suffering or enduring. Passion is such a strong emotion or affection it's been said that it is "at its core, a form of pain that demands it be quenched."[3]

When I think of people who exhibit the passion to pursue their dreams, I think of Dr. Martin Luther King, Jr.'s hope for freedom and equal rights; my husband's desire to help children who are victims of divorce, violence, and absent parents; and Mother Teresa's passionate love and service to those living in poverty. I also think of my friend who *can't not* travel the state training people to help those who have been victims of sex trafficking, and a pastor who tears up when expressing the needs of hungry children.

Passion gives each of these people drive and continued commitment. Their passion pushes them forward. It comes from within. And, it draws them and leads others into service through careers, ministry, and purposeful living.

Other passions may include hobbies or interests such as gardening, bicycling, solving puzzles, baking, running marathons, or writing. These passions may bring you and others happiness. They, too, can be the origin or part of a service, career, or ministry, and a door to life change in self and others.

Identifying your passions and including them in your life is key to living your HeartSong.

God guards knowledge with a passion.

—Proverbs 22:12 (MSG)

When you think of people who follow their passions, who comes to mind?

_____

_____

_____

What adjectives would you use to describe these people of passion? *(Besides passionate!)*

_____

_____

_____

What causes are you most passionate about? What injustices make your blood boil hottest? What makes your heart break and brings you to tears? Whom do you feel drawn to help most? What hobbies bring you delight?

Example:

My passion: I have an inward push to encourage others and help them know and live believing God's truth about their worth, their power to overcome, and their destiny.

What brings me to tears: People and animals who feel or are trapped and want to break free but don't know how.

The injustice that makes my blood boil most: Deception, human trafficking, and animal cruelty.

I am drawn to help: Those who want to transform their lives.

I enjoy these hobbies: Bicycling, walking, yoga, entertaining, crafting, singing, piano playing, baking.

How these passions are incorporated into my life: These passions are incorporated into my work as a professional life coach and by volunteering my coaching services at a local non-profit, serving to end sex trafficking of minors, helping lead worship, adopting our pets, making time to be creative, enjoying exercise and the outdoors, entertaining…always including something baked.

While you and I may not forever serve in the same roles within the same organizations, to live our most fulfilling and purposed lives, our passions must always be woven into our days.

> He…wrapped himself in a cloak of divine passion.
>
> —Isaiah 59:17

Now it's your turn!

What inward push do you feel most passionately?

_____

_____

_____

What breaks your heart most? Brings you to tears?

_____

_____

_____

What injustice makes your blood boil most?

_____

_____

_____

What are your favorite hobbies?

_____

_____

_____

How have your passions been incorporated into the roles and activities of your life?

_____

_____

_____

Do you believe your dream and God's purpose for your life relate to your inner drives and passions? Explain.

_____

_____

_____

Every great dream begins with a dreamer.
Always remember, you have within you the strength, the patience,
and the passion to reach for the stars to change the world.

—Harriet Tubman

Identifying your passions
and including them
in your life
is key to living your HeartSong.

HEART CHALLENGE 5

Loving Through Service

In the end, the number of prayers we say
may contribute to our happiness,
but the number of prayers we answer may
be of even greater importance.

—Dieter F. Uchtdorf

If you believe God and his teaching, then you also believe love, grace, and service are inseparable. God provided the ultimate example of His loving grace through Christ's service.

God loved the world so much that He gave...

—John 3:16 (NCV)

Throughout Jesus's time on earth, he taught in word and deed that love is service.

I was hungry and you gave me food, I was thirsty and you gave me something to drink, I was a stranger and you welcomed me.

—Matthew 25:35 (NRSV)

Later, Paul carried this important message to the church—and to us:

But I will rejoice even if I lose my life pouring it out like a liquid offering to God, just like your faithful service is an offering to God. And I want all of you to share that joy.

—Philippians 2:17

What Does It Mean to Give?

When my husband and I were first married, we heard, as God would have it, a sermon on that very topic—marriage. I don't remember a lot of what the pastor said, but these few words from his message were illuminated and have stayed with both of us to this day. *"Marriage is a giving game."*

What we both understood the pastor to say was this: *love* is a giving game. So, whether or not you're married, this story applies. Keep reading!

When we heard these words, something clicked. Never mind my husband gets very serious about winning anything that sounds, looks, or smells like a competition. So, he took the idea of winning the giving game as a personal challenge, which has been a very good thing for me!

I'm not quite so competitive, but God did begin opening my eyes to the fact that real love—love for him, love for myself, love for my husband, and love for others has everything to do with sacrificing self because of what, in God's grace, he sacrificed for me.

Sacrificing for my husband, kids, and friends is one thing. It's not always easy, but doable, transformative, and ultimately so worth it. But sacrificing my time, gifts, and talents beyond my inner circle to those I kind of, sort of, know or don't know at all is quite another. It's still doable, transformative, and worth it. But, somehow, it can also be more difficult.

This defining moment of choice between service and self is where the rubber meets the road. Which path will you choose to travel? Robert Frost teaches us the road you take *makes all the difference*. It makes a difference to your life and the lives of so many others.

Jesus showed us how to choose the road of service all the way to the cross. He became undeserved love in action. Sacrificing. Giving. Serving. And in the end—pure joy. Joy in the service and joy for the recipients of his giving.

Here's a thought. What if Jesus had chosen self over the cross? We can only imagine. Actually, we probably cannot. What we do know for sure is that when our acts of loving service go missing, fulfillment and joy go missing as well.

> I slept and I dreamed that life is all joy.
> I woke and I saw that life is all service.
> I served and I saw that service is joy.
>
> —Mother Teresa

What Areas of Service are Written on Your Heart?

Think back. Recall, and list as many areas of service from your past as you can according to life stage.

Childhood (0–12)

_____

_____

_____

Teen Years (13–19)

_____

_____

_____

Young Adult (20–35)

_____

_____

_____

Middle Age (36–51)

_____

_____

_____

Maturity (52 →)

_____

_____

_____

What areas of service did and do you enjoy most? Least?

_____

_____

_____

Are there people you might like to serve you've not yet helped?

_____

_____

_____

Are you willing to serve in this area? If so, how and when will you take your first step? If not, why not?

_____

_____

_____

The only thing that counts is faith expressing itself through love.

—Galatians 5:6 (NIV)

...when acts of loving
service go missing, fulfillment and joy
go missing as well.

HEART CHALLENGE 6

The Melody of Your Heart

When the songs of your heart
start singing, you should listen...
for its harmony will
bring you happiness
and the melody is the voice
of your true spirit.

—Paulo Coelho

Your Melody

God set you apart to sing a melody. Have you begun to sense the tune and rhythm of your song?

All this time, through every page, he has been preparing you to boldly share your voice with others.

You've answered many thought-provoking and prayer-inducing questions on *Your HeartSong Journey*. Now, it's time to review and look closely for what God has been teaching you.

Indeed, he loves his people; all his holy ones are in his hands.
They follow in his steps and accept his teaching.

—Deuteronomy 33:3

Review your responses to each Heart Challenge question you've completed to this point: All of Step One (seven challenges), all of Step Two (twelve challenges), and much of Step Three (five challenges).

As you go through and reread your answers, highlight the words, phrases, and lessons you find resonate with you most in each challenge. Then, write what you've highlighted under the corresponding Heart Challenge below. This is important!

Step One
Your True Identity and Sacred Worth

Good Enough—Loved No Matter What

Heart Challenges

1. Identifying Your Current Life Scenario

_____

_____

_____

2. Who Do You Say You Are?

_____

_____

_____

3. Who Does God Say You Are?

_____

_____

_____

4. Chosen, Not Compared

_____

_____

_____

5. Always Good Enough

_____

_____

_____

6. Self-Love

_____

_____

_____

7. Lavished in Love, Not Pride or Shame

_____

_____

_____

Step Two
Break Free From What
Holds You Back

Overcoming Obstacles—Building Character

Heart Challenges

1. Your Values

_____

_____

_____

2. Your Priorities

_____

_____

_____

3. Your Roles and Life Balance

_____

_____

_____

4. Your Mindset

_____

_____

_____

5. Conquering Your Thought Life

_____

_____

_____

6. Christ-Like Character Traits

_____

_____

_____

7. Identifying Your Character Strengths

_____

_____

_____

8. What is Your Motivation?

_____

_____

_____

9. Overcoming Fear

_____

_____

_____

10. Your Grief Matters

_____

_____

_____

11. Forgiving and Living

_____

_____

_____

12. Habits and Attitudes

_____

_____

_____

Step Three
Casting Your Dream.
Claiming Your Purpose.
Taking Action.

Moving Forward as God Leads

Heart Challenges

1. Discerning Your Spiritual Gifts

_____

_____

_____

2. Be Inspired

_____

_____

_____

3. Remembering Your Success

_____

_____

_____

4. Your Passions

_____

_____

_____

5. Loving Through Service

_____

_____

_____

Review the highlighted words, phrases, and messages you've just written under each Heart Challenge. Find the ones repeated in steps one, two, and three. Write them here.

_____

_____

_____

_____

_____

What do you believe God has been teaching you?

_____

_____

_____

_____

_____

_____

_____

In one sentence, write what you sense the Holy Spirit is speaking to your heart right now.

_____

_____

_____

Some stand on tiptoe trying to reach God to talk—
you try too hard, friend—drop to your knees
and listen, he'll hear you better that way.

—Terri Guillemets

God set you apart
to sing a melody…
he has been preparing you to boldly
share your voice with others.

HEART CHALLENGE 7

Clarifying Your God-Given Message

Sing, I tell you,
and all the angels will sing with you!

—Suzy Kassem

The way God made you, your unique experiences, choices, and challenges, people and places, responsibilities and roles, thoughts and actions, and more have shaped who you are today. They were meant to draw you ever closer to Christ for a purpose whether you knew he was near or not.

It's time to begin discerning that purpose by first identifying the message God has written on your heart. Your unique and heartfelt message provides the lyrics to your song—the one he asks you to share in the way only you can.

Your Message

Look deep into your heart. Based on what you've learned from the Holy Spirit's guidance through the previous pages, what do you want people to know more than anything?

_____

_____

_____

With whom do you believe you are meant to share this message?

_____

_____

_____

A reliable messenger brings healing.

—Proverbs 13:17

How and where do you think God wants you to share your message?

_____

_____

_____

What other details can you share about your message?

_____

_____

_____

Visualize yourself sharing your message. How do you feel as you see yourself sharing your message?

_____

_____

_____

How do people respond to your message in your vision?

_____

_____

_____

Do you think Jesus cares whether or not you share this message? Why or why not?

_____

_____

_____

Your message, your ministry, your influence is built from your flaws. People relate to humanity … not perfection.

—Mandy Hale

Your unique and heartfelt
message provides the lyrics
to your song—the one he asks you
to share in the way only you can.

HEART CHALLENGE 8

Your Credo

A credo is a statement of faith. In this case, it's what you believe about:

- Your identity and sacred worth.
- Breaking through what holds you back.
- Your message.

In a moment, you'll write your own credo. Just for fun, find the song below on YouTube. I hope you'll be inspired as you listen to this music and begin writing your own credo on the following page.

"This I Believe (The Creed)" by Hillsong Worship[4]

Example: Gail's Credo

I believe I am: Who God says I am—his beloved child. I believe God sees me—and has forgiven me. I believe the Holy Spirit fills me. I am empowered by the Holy Spirit to do the heart-work and hard work it takes to boldly live the life of joy, peace, and purpose God intends.

I believe I can break through what holds me back by: Staying in fellowship with God and in his word early and often each day; praising and praying scripture and confessing what the Holy Spirit puts on my heart; standing firm and by his grace, experiencing the transformation of my mind and my heart by his power and love.

I believe the message God desires I share is: In Christ, you are good enough and loved no matter what, you can break free from what holds you back, and God has a purpose for your life you're meant to live.

Make a careful examination of who you are and the work you've been given, and then sink yourself into that.

—Galatians 6:4 (MSG)

My Credo

I believe I am…(express your worth)

_____

_____

_____

_____

I believe I can break through what holds me back by…
(how you will overcome)

_____

_____

I believe the message God desires I share is…(what, to whom, when, where)

Do not fear, only believe.

—Mark 5:36 (ESV)

I believe I am who God says I am.
I believe I can break through what
holds me back. I believe God has
a message for me to share.

HEART CHALLENGE 9

Casting Your Dream and Claiming Your Purpose

My dreams had to be His dreams, the ones He placed in my heart. They couldn't be the ones I thought I should have, or needed for the purpose of making other people like me.

—Stormie Omartian

Today is the day. The right time is now to cast your inspired dream.

Casting your dream is a bit like fishing. When you fish, you cast your line, and you let it fly so you can gather in the fish.

You feel a tug. You struggle to bring it in. You keep the fish or release it.

Casting your dream is not so different. You open the door of your mind to the godly thoughts and desires that tug most at your heart. Then…

➢ You name your dream.
➢ You decide the struggle is too great and you discard it, or
➢ You keep and intentionally pursue your dream.

Whatever you decide, know this; unlike fish that scatter when released, your inspired dream remains forever in your heart waiting to be captured, reeled in, and lived.

> Many men go fishing all of their lives without knowing
> it is not fish they are after.
>
> —Henry David Thoreau

Cast Your Dream

Today, you're the dream caster. No idea or godly intention is too absurd or large. Nothing of good repute is out of bounds as you ask the Holy Spirit to guide you toward, to reveal to you, or to remind you of (or confirm) the dream God has given you.

You have been given a dream just as God gave one to Joseph (Read Genesis 37:5–7,9). Just as Joseph's dream was fulfilled, Genesis 41:39–44, so is yours meant to be! So, cast your inspired dream far and wide. You may struggle with this a little at first, but go ahead—ask God to give you a glimpse of his dream for your life. Allow yourself to feel the excitement of what you are about to reel in!

> Hope deferred makes the heart sick,
> But a dream fulfilled is a tree of life.
>
> —Proverbs 13:12

Begin dream casting with God by asking and answering these two questions.

1. *What kind of person do you most want to be?*

It's been said: Our doing is based on our being. What kind of person do you most want to be so you can do what you've been called to do?

_____

_____

_____

2. *What dream do you believe God has given you?*

Josh Eddy shares a deep, abiding truth we are meant to consider when naming our dream. "To surrender a precious dream is a fearful thing, but to pursue anything but the full measure of God's love is a wasted life." What dream has *God* placed on your heart?

_____

_____

_____

How do you envision your *being* impacting and leading to your *doing*—living your God-given dream?

_____

_____

_____

"You could rattle the stars," she whispered.
"You could do anything, if only you dared.
And deep down you know it, too.
That's what scares you most."

—Sarah J. Maas, *Throne of Glass*

Claim Your Purpose

Purpose does not replace your deep need to draw near to your Father—drawing near is the only way to accomplish it.

You are near the end of *Your HeartSong Journey*. This next step will help you clarify God's purpose for your life, the thing he created you to accomplish as only you can.

You've been given a message and you've cast your dream. Now, it's time to determine how this dream is woven into your destiny and whom you are called to serve. But before you do, there's something you should know: While your circumstances, roles, and seasons in life change, God hasn't and doesn't. He nailed down his purpose and plan for you long ago. So, even as we go and grow, we can be sure our God-designed purpose is steadfast. The responsibilities, titles, and jobs we have may change but not our most important and influential calling. In these next scriptures, you'll see how good God is about guiding us to realize our special purpose by example.

Here's what I mean.

Scriptural Guidance to Purpose

God provides many examples of biblical characters whose purpose he revealed to us. Moses, Mary, Joseph, Esther, Zechariah, Hannah, and many more. Here are three scriptures from the Old and

New Testament that highlight the distinct purposes of Jeremiah and Paul (previously known as Saul).

In the Old Testament book of Jeremiah, the Lord tells Jeremiah the following:

> I knew you before I formed you in your mother's womb. Before you were born I set you apart and appointed you as my prophet to the nations.
>
> —Jeremiah 1:5 (NIV)

In the New Testament book of Acts, the apostle Paul (Saul) recounts the story of Jesus stopping him on the road to Damascus. Among other things, Jesus shares with Saul God's calling on his life. He tells Saul to whom he is called and declares Saul's purpose.

> I have appeared to you to appoint you as a servant and as a witness of what you have seen of me and will see of me. I will rescue you from your own people and from the Gentiles. I am sending you to them to open their eyes and turn them from darkness to light, and from the power of Satan to God, so that they may receive forgiveness of sins and a place among those who are sanctified by faith in me.
>
> —Acts 26:16–18 (NIV)

The Bible also records Paul himself, speaking to the Galatians and explaining to them God's purpose for his life, whom God called him to serve, and what he was to accomplish. This is what Paul said.

But even before I was born, God chose me and called me by his marvelous grace. Then it pleased him to reveal his Son to me, so that I would proclaim the Good News about Jesus to the Gentiles.

—Galatians 1:15–16

Keeping God's confirmation to Jeremiah, Jesus's declaration to Saul, and Paul's words to the Galatians in mind, and taking into consideration your…

> ➢ true identity and sacred worth,
> ➢ power to overcome,
> ➢ strengths,
> ➢ spiritual gifts,
> ➢ values,
> ➢ good habits,
> ➢ passions,
> ➢ successes,
> ➢ interests in serving,
> ➢ message,
> ➢ credo, and
> ➢ dream…

…it's time to claim your purpose.

One final and important thing to note: We all fall under the same large umbrella purpose of bringing glory to God as we go about our lives in his image spreading the Good News and making disciples (Matthew 28:18–20). When you look closely, you see within this *Great Commission* there is a special mission to which you are called as a unique individual, a distinct purpose God created you to complete as only you can…in the *time* and *place* he appointed you to live.

From one man he made every nation of men, that they
should inhabit the whole earth; and he determined
the times set for them and the exact places
where they should live.

—Acts 17:25-26

When we determine times and exact places it's for good reason. Don't you think it's even truer of our great God? There can be no doubt, *you have a significant reason for being here and now.* Like the disciples, your reason greatly impacts the lives of others and brings glory to God!

To claim your purpose, begin by breaking it down step-by-step into a statement. As you write, remember this: *Your purpose statement is influenced by your inspired dream.* Together, this is your HeartSong.

Following God's example in Jeremiah 1:5, Acts 26:16-18 and Galatians 1:15-16, here is my purpose statement.

> *God has set me apart and appointed me as an encourager, guide, and truth-teller to those who sense something is missing and feel like they're meant for more, by helping them break free from what holds them back so they can discover the love and hope found in knowing and living God's dream and purpose for their lives according to his plan.*

Ask the Holy Spirit to guide you as together you complete your HeartSong purpose statement below.

God has set me apart and appointed me to serve (as what?) _____

_____

to (whom?)

_____

by (doing what?)

_____

so they (do/become what?)

_____

Be sure to thank God and share with your coach, partner, or group your excitement about what he has revealed to you!

The two most important days in your life are the day you are born and the day you find out why.

—Mark Twain

While your circumstances, roles,
and seasons in life change,
God hasn't and doesn't. He nailed down
his purpose and plan for you long ago.

HEART
CHALLENGE 10

Pause to Surrender

This letter is from Paul, a slave of Christ Jesus,
chosen by God to be an apostle and sent
out to preach his Good News.

—Romans 1:1

What a journey you've traveled! You've learned and overcome much. And while discovering your HeartSong is ultra-gratifying and quite profound it is all useless until you surrender your will to God's. Surrender is always the forerunner to meaning and fulfillment.

A New Life of Purpose Requires Surrender

Notice in the scripture above what comes first; *Paul, a slave of Christ Jesus*. Then, *chosen by God to be an apostle and sent out to preach his Good News*. First, surrender. Then, a new life living out his calling.

To live our HeartSong, we must first surrender. So, let's discuss surrender. What is it? *Merriam-Webster* defines surrender as *yielding power, control or possession.* I surrender some? No. For the follower of Christ, it's *I surrender all.* It's giving up the old, natural self—the, I'll do it my way self—to Christ. When we accept Jesus as our Savior, our loving Father gifts us his very character. As we believe and trust him, we make room to grow his life in us by allowing him to pour out through our special qualities. You remain you and I remain me in our uniqueness, but as believers, it's Christ that lives in and through us to the degree we allow him to shine.[5]

We witness this truth as Jesus gave himself up all the way to the cross. How else but by the strength of God could Jesus have submitted to the humiliation and pain of this brutal tree? His human self would have fought against it. Instead, his spiritual self completed his mission as only he could.

You and I are called to surrender ourselves—to become bound as slaves to the gift of Christ within us. John the Baptist says it this way: "He must become greater and greater, and I must become less and less." As it was for John, this expanding of Christ happens by our choice. By the power of his Spirit whispering to us, and our choosing to trust him and follow.

Sadly, I'll have to admit, the Holy Spirit has had to repeat himself *maybe* once or twice (or more) before I listened. And obeying my Master? That's been a long, hard, circular road at times. But as I've come to know Jesus more, I've chosen to surrender to his ways in the moments of my days more often. Don't get me wrong. Letting go is not always that easy. But it could be. Why? My old self already died with Christ on the cross. I just keep choosing to revive it! Yet, Jesus speaks to me as I seek his help in the battle between mine and his—the old life and the new. He is there directing and providing for me as the best of masters do. And then I choose. Will I stay in the old life where I'm comfortable and used to its trappings? Or will I live in my new life? The one he died to give me. The one that fits me like a glove and brings me joy I've never known. The one I deep down so desperately crave?

How about you? Will you surrender to Christ who lives in you?

> My old self has been crucified with Christ. It is no longer I who live, but Christ lives in me. So I live in this earthly body by trusting in the Son of God, who loved me and gave himself for me.
>
> —Galatians 2:20

Will You Choose to Be a Slave of Christ?

This is what pastor and author Kyle Idleman wrote in his book, *Not a Fan*.

> When we accept the invitation to deny ourselves and follow Jesus, we become his slaves. That's a completely different way to look at slavery. We think of slavery as something we're forced into, but Jesus invites us to deny ourselves. Why would anyone ever want to be a slave? Actually, it was rare, but in the Old Testament we read of people who chose to be slaves. They were called "Bond Slaves." These were people who were set free after being a slave for six years, but they decided they wanted to stay a slave. (Deuteronomy 15:16–17).... A bondslave is how many of the New

Testament writers describe themselves. They had willingly become slaves. Luke chapter 1 tells us that when Mary heard that she would be giving birth to the Messiah, her response (recorded in verse 38) is, "I am the Lord's servant." But the word is "bondslave."[6]

Jesus said, "If anyone wants to be my follower, you must turn from your selfish ways, take up your cross daily, and follow me" (Luke 9:23). Our HeartSong can't be lived in the old life. It can only be lived each day in the new life of surrender. So, I ask, are you willing to give up self and serve Christ? Is it your heart's desire to surrender all moment-by-moment to gain the new life you long to live?

By his divine power, God has given us everything
we need for living a godly life.

—2 Peter 1:3

Prayer of Surrender
My sacrifice, O God, is a broken spirit;
a broken and contrite heart you, God, will not despise.

—Psalm 51:17

Before going any further, reflect once more on all God has revealed to you about your true identity and how you can boldly live in this truth because of his mercy, grace, and never-ending love. Then, when you're ready, with a Christ-like attitude of humble, loving obedience, draw near to God and willingly surrender all.

A prayer of surrender is written below to help you. Speak it aloud as it is or write and say a prayer of your own before taking the next step to act on and begin living your HeartSong.

Father,

You created me just as you desired me. You loved the idea of me. You gave me your very breath. But here I am a combination of stubborn will, wanderings, brokenness, and cravings. I confess I have tried to do things my way. I haven't listened to you even when I cried out for answers. I've chosen instead to let the ways of the world, accusations, and my pride fill my mind and drown out your voice.

I've been afraid. Afraid of loss, judgment, rejection, responsibility, failure, and not being good enough. I've doubted you, Jesus. I've not trusted you to show me the way. Now, the burden of needing to be in control has brought me to my knees.

I lay all of that—and every bit of me—at the cross because you have been calling me to something more…more of you.

You cover and enfold me in your love, holding me there in the palm of your hand where you have written my name. You have given me everything. Life, breath, work, protection, sustenance, guidance. You have cherished every tear. You have died. All for me.

I am in awe and cling to your Presence. I surrender, Lord. I surrender my moments, hours, days, dreams—my life to you. I desire to serve you alone.

For now, I am certain that it is only in your unfailing grace and by the power of your Spirit that I can boldly live with joy, peace, and faith the song you have written on my heart—the one I am desperate to sing for you.

In Jesus's name I pray. Amen.

Will I stay in the old life
where I'm comfortable and used to its
trappings?
Or will I live in my new life?
The one he died to give me?

HEART
CHALLENGE 11

Your Action Plan

God has put a dream inside you. It is yours, and no one else's.
It declares your uniqueness. It holds your potential.
Only you can birth it. Only you can live it.
Not to discover it, take responsibility for it,
and act upon it is to negatively affect
yourself as well as all those
who would benefit from
your dream.

—John C. Maxwell

You have surrendered—told God you give up your will, ways, and purposes to him. What's left to do? *Go! Take action!*

Knowing your HeartSong brings the responsibility of living it. And as you dare to step out in faith, you impact the lives of others as only you can. The result? Your most fulfilling, influential, and God-glorifying life.

To do this, you need a plan. God's step-by-step plan.

Jesus hasn't led us to this place to make our dreams come true.
Our dreams, just like the disciples' are always too
small. We're here to fulfill God's dream that will bring
him glory through a remarkably abundant life.

—Bruce Wilkinson

Preparing For Action

When Nehemiah, King Artaxerxes's cupbearer and a Jew, heard the news that the walls of Jerusalem had been torn down (Nehemiah 1:4–11), he was concerned about God's people and the trouble and disgrace the broken-down walls would bring upon them, their holy city, and the temple.

Once Nehemiah learned of the needs of God's people, his heart was broken. He wept, fasted, and prayed. Then, he acted—one step at a time.

With God, you have determined your HeartSong, cast your dream, and claimed your purpose. You discovered whom you are to serve, proclaimed what you will do to serve them, and revealed the benefit they will receive through your service.

Now, like Nehemiah, it's time to pour out your heart to God, repent, fast as you are led, pray, praise, and give thanks. Make specific requests like Nehemiah did. Then, you will be ready to commit to the step-by-step action plan God puts on your heart.

I never worry about action, but only inaction.

—Winston Churchill

God's Plan for You

And this is God's plan: Both Gentiles and Jews who believe the
Good News share equally in the riches inherited by God's children.
Both are of the same body, and both enjoy the promise of the
blessings because they belong to Christ Jesus.
By God's grace and mighty power, I have been given the
privilege of serving him by spreading this Good News.

—Ephesians 3:6–7

God likes a good plan. He has one. It's called his Master Plan.
He works it with the finished product in mind. Everything he does,
allows, and creates is woven into this plan for his purposes and
toward new life.

God shaped, chose, and called Paul to work within his plan
by spreading the Good News to the Gentiles. I hope by now you've
embraced, in the deepest recesses of your heart, the truth that you are
designed, selected, and appointed to serve in a unique and specific
part of his plan, too.

As you write your action plan, it's worth remembering Jesus's
words: *My yoke is easy to bear, and the burden I give you is light*
(Matthew 11:30). Your HeartSong (and God's plan for you to live it)
is not meant to be complicated. It's simple, meaningful, productive,
and purposeful.

Begin writing your plan on the following page. Find a quiet
place where you can be alone with God and without interruption for
as long as it takes you to finish. Enter this time with thanksgiving
and worship—even fasting (See Acts 13:2). Read scripture. Meditate.
Pray. Wait on the Lord to lead, then write. The idea is to seek God's
will and his predetermined steps for you, not force your personal
agenda.

Finally, the most humbling of truths is this: God has no need for you or me to fulfill his purposes for him. He could, if he chose to, bring his plan to completion without us. But he has invited you and me to, above all, know him more and go with him as he fulfills his plan through us. Draw close to him now. Do not be compelled to set random goals. Wait on him. Ask him to show you only the next loving and purpose-filled steps of his plan.

"For I know the plans I have for you," says the Lord.
"They are plans for good and not for disaster, to give
you a future and a hope. In those days when you pray, I
will listen. If you look for me wholeheartedly, you will
find me. I will be found by you," says the Lord.

—Jeremiah 29:11-12

Your HeartSong (and God's plan for you to live it) is not meant to be complicated. It's simple, meaningful, productive, and purposeful.

Your HeartSong Journey

Action Plan

_____*(Date)*

Commit your actions to the Lord, and your plans will succeed.

—Proverbs 16:3

Prelude to Your Action Plan

➢ Begin by rewriting your HeartSong purpose statement from page 214–15:

_____

_____

_____

_____

_____

➢ What scripture or quote inspires you to live your HeartSong?

_____

_____

_____

_____

_____

➢ Describe the reality of you living your HeartSong today.

_____

_____

_____

_____

_____

➢ Describe your *best* vision of living your HeartSong.

_____

_____

_____

_____

_____

Write down this vision and clearly inscribe it.

—Habakkuk 2:2 (NAS)

➢ What needs to change for you to move from your current reality to your *best* vision of living your HeartSong?

_____

_____

_____

_____

_____

➢ What unique position are you in or do you hold that strengthens and influences your ability to move forward in your HeartSong? (As the king's cupbearer, Nehemiah had direct contact with the king. Nehemiah 1:11)

_____

_____

_____

_____

➢ What personal relationships, resources, and leverage do you have that can assist you in fulfilling your HeartSong? Whom can you tell? (In time, Nehemiah spoke to the priests, nobles, officials, and others on the administration about the plan God put on his heart. Nehemiah 2:16–17)

_____

_____

_____

➤ What will it mean to you to live into your HeartSong as you go about your days?

_____

_____

_____

➤ What will your mindset and thoughts need to be for you to confidently, courageously, and intentionally live your HeartSong?

_____

_____

_____

➤ Whom will you influence for Christ as you live your HeartSong?

_____

_____

_____

Trust in the Lord with all your heart and lean not
on your own understanding; in all your ways submit
to him and he will make your paths straight.

—Psalm 3:5–6 (NIV)

➤ Describe who you will have become at the end of your life having lived your HeartSong.

_____

_____

_____

➤ What legacy do you hope to leave? How will you be remembered having lived your HeartSong?

_____

_____

_____

➤ Take time to ponder and meditate on your responses. Write any additional thoughts that come to mind.

_____

_____

_____

God's master-plan is made up of our individual assignments whose collective objective is to impact mankind positively.

—D.S. Mashego

The Steps of Your Action Plan

The story of Nehemiah is one of faith and restoration. It began with a prayer and a vision and ended with new life for God's people. But, all this required a faithful servant and a plan. Today, you are that faithful servant. God has given you his vision for your life—your HeartSong. It suits you and his purposes perfectly. Now, *with God*, create your step-by-step action plan. Then, commit to following through and taking God and his dream, purpose, and plan for your life seriously. In God's time and like his chosen people you, too, will see your new life beginning.

➢ *Determine one to three action steps to begin living your HeartSong.*

Action Step 1

_____

Action Step 2

_____

Action Step 3

_____

➢ *How is each step meaningful to living your HeartSong?*

Action Step 1

_____

Action Step 2

_____

Action Step 3

_____

➢ *How will each step be accomplished? What will you need to do? Who and what is involved? Get specific!*

Action Step 1

_____

Action Step 2

_____

Action Step 3

_____

➤ *Determine a beginning and completion date for each action step. At least one step should be begin today.*

Action Step 1

_____

Action Step 2

_____

Action Step 3

_____

> On that day, on the very final day of our lives,
> what will we hope we decided to do on this one?
>
> —Gregg McKeown

Congratulations! With God, you've discovered your HeartSong and now have a plan to begin living it!

Remember this, your action plan is a living document. Use and review it with God each day. As you move through each inspired and intentional step, look from a heavenly perspective at what he is accomplishing in and through you. Once this plan and its steps are complete, copy the blank *Next Step Action Plan* provided at the end of this book so you can keep stepping forward to see your inspired dream and God-designed purpose thrive.

Be forewarned. It's easy to start with enthusiasm and then drift away. Be intentional! *Do Not Give Up!* The world will want you to stop. The enemy will want you to doubt and become discouraged.

But you, when you feel those things, capture your thoughts and exchange them for truth. Sink into God's love and be determined to risk letting Jesus take you where he's calling you to go in his timing and on his pathway.

> The Lord will work out his plans for my life—
> For your faithful love, O Lord, endures forever.
>
> —Psalm 138:8

Here are ten tips to help you stay the course and work through your God-inspired action plan:

1. *Commit your way to the Lord* each morning. Praise him. Repent of and turn away from sin as you go about your days.
2. *Remember who God says you are.* Choose to think on those things so you can live like you believe him.
3. *Accept his love and grace with thankfulness* as he grows you in character, confidence, strength, and holiness.
4. *Ask the Holy Spirit to guide you* as you live the moments of your day. Pay attention to his promptings. Follow him in humble obedience. No grumbling.
5. *Find an accountability partner* to encourage and hold you responsible to fulfill your action steps. This is important! (Hint: Spouses normally do not make the best accountability partners. Seek a coach or faithful friend.)
6. *Guard your mind taking every thought captive to Christ—* the truth! Study, meditate on, and discuss scripture with others!
7. *Stand firm in faith.* Discuss any obstacles with God and your accountability partner. Pray with your partner.

8. *Journal* about what God is revealing and teaching you.
9. *Add new steps* as you complete each one and as the Holy Spirit leads.
10. *Be patient. Live surrendered. Enjoy your journey and growing relationship with Christ.* Allow God to use your circumstances—he is working out his marvelous purpose and plan for your life for his glory, your good, and the benefit of others!

Sink into God's love
and be determined to risk
letting Jesus take you
where he's calling you to go.

HEART
CHALLENGE 12

Your Testimony

Living your HeartSong and working your plan requires courageous, bold, and intentional faith. Faith that believes the One who created you and loves you is in you and for you. Faith the Holy Spirit will lead, protect, and flow through you as you allow. Recall this:

> Abraham never wavered in believing God's promise.
> In fact, his faith grew stronger, and in this he brought glory to God.
> Fully convinced that God is able to do whatever he promises.
> And because of Abraham's faith, God counted
> him as righteous. And when God counted him as
> righteous it wasn't just for Abraham's benefit.
>
> —Romans 4:20–23

This is your burning bush moment—your anointing. Listen to God closely as he shares his heart. *I will give you the faith of Abraham if you will open your heart to receive it. You are mine. I will lead you through the waters to the mountaintop where I will reward you for a job well done. I love you. I am with you. Come. Follow me. Others need what you have to offer. This is the way you are meant to go.*

It's time to testify to your Holy Spirit-driven faith as you boldly begin your new life of purpose.

By Faith, I Testify…

- I am God's idea, his child, and I belong to him.
- Because of God's deep love and Christ's willing sacrifice, I am good enough, brave enough, just plain *enough*, to answer and fulfill my calling.
- I am loved no matter what.
- My sins have been forgiven, and I am growing in Christ's character as he prepares and works through me to fulfill my mission.
- I have been called and set apart to do significant Kingdom work.
- God has given me an inspired dream and unique purpose I alone am meant to live.
- God has a plan for me to accomplish his purpose for my life according to his will.
- I have been given and accept the authority and power of the Holy Spirit to accomplish God's purpose through me, and I will do my part. For my God is with me, therefore I will not be distracted, and I will not let fear stop me.

Read Hebrews 11:1-11. Then, write your own *by faith* statement relative to living your HeartSong.

By faith I…

_____

_____

_____

_____

_____

_____

_____

_____

_____

Now that you have received what God has revealed to you and you have chosen to live by faith with all the power and authority of Christ already given to you, *go*. Be intentional. Glorify God and benefit others in Christ as you move with him through your days to accomplish his dream and purpose for your life. There, together with Jesus in the midst of your HeartSong, you'll experience the new life you crave and are meant to live.

I love you. I am with you.
Come. Follow me.
Others need what you have to offer.
This is the way you are meant to go.

EPILOGUE

Glory to God for the Good Things He Has Planned for You!

For we are God's masterpiece. He created us anew in Christ
Jesus, so we can do the good things he planned for us long ago.

—Ephesians 2:10

You've come to the end of *Your HeartSong Journey*! You've done the
hard work and placed one foot in front of the other on this road
to self-worth, strength, and purpose. You've likely been humbled,
encouraged, and changed by what the Lord has revealed to you along
your way. You've even proclaimed your personal Holy Spirit-driven
faith by your testimony. And I trust you've drawn closer to Christ
and discovered the hope found in knowing and believing:

- The truth of your identity and sacred worth,
- You can break free from what holds you back, and
- God has a purpose and plan for your life.

Your next step is to be faithful to live out your action plan—the one the Holy Spirit spoke to your heart so you can complete the good things God has planned for you.

Notice, as shown on the previous page in Ephesians 2:10, God says we *can* do the good things he planned for us.

If you believe God, then you must believe this scripture is truth spoken not only for everyone around you, but to you specifically: *You can* do the things he planned for you because he is always with you and his Spirit will complete them through you as you live surrendered to his will.

You can choose to stay comfortable and, I hate to say it, less than faithful to God's calling. You might even be indecisive about moving forward. But, here's something you need to know about indecision: Indecision *is* a decision—a decision to do nothing. Indecision is a swirling merry-go-round of empty space where fear and doubt take turns leading. Unfortunately, I've learned this by experience. But the cross proves we're meant for more. We're meant to find joy in our moments. Not fret over them. God is ever-giving us the opportunity to change and bless as we go. Not on our own. With Christ. Our feet are meant for walking by way of faith. They're not designed to keep us spinning in a world of me-filled uncertainty.

What happens when we choose to do nothing with the gifts, talents, and resources God has given? Well, remember the parable of the talents?

To those who use well what they are given, even more will
be given, and they will have abundance. But from those who
do nothing, even what little they have will be taken away.

—Matthew 25:29

The better choice? Stand firm believing the truth that *you can* do the things God has prepared for you to do in and through Christ. *You can* and are born to live into your HeartSong and enjoy your new life as he lives and bears fruit through you!

In his book, *As a Man Thinketh*, inspirational author James Allen, writes, "Having conceived of our purpose, we should mentally make out a straight pathway to its achievement, looking neither to the right nor the left."[7]

My friend, be decided you belong to God. Choose to live your moments believing in Christ that you are already good enough and loved no matter what. Know in his victory, you are an overcomer today and tomorrow. Give thanks by his grace he has revealed and you have received his unique message, dream, and purpose for your life…and the power of his Spirit within you to complete it.

Finally, be encouraged. Stay the course. Your inspired action plan is your straight pathway to the something more you seek. Don't look to the right or to the left. Don't stay frozen in time but move according to God's direction. Dare to step forward with Christ into your new life. Dare to live the song God has written on your heart.

Now to him who is able to do immeasurably more than all we ask or imagine, according to his power that is at work within us, to him be the glory in the church and in Christ Jesus throughout all generations, for ever and ever! Amen.

—Ephesians 3:20–21

Dare to step forward with Christ
into your new life.
Dare to live the song
God has written on your heart.

NEXT STEP ACTION PLAN

_____ *(Date)*

Write your HeartSong purpose statement

_____

_____

_____

_____

     Prayerfully determine your next one to three Holy Spirit-led action steps to continue living into your HeartSong.

Action Step 1 _____

Action Step 2 _____

Action Step 3 _____

➤ How is each step meaningful to living your HeartSong?

Action Step 1 _____

Action Step 2 _____

Action Step 3 _____

➤ **How will each step be accomplished? What will you need to do?**
Who and what is involved? Get specific!

Action Step 1 _____

Action Step 2 _____

Action Step 3 _____

➤ **Determine a beginning and completion date for each action step.**

Action Step 1 _____

Action Step 2 _____

Action Step 3 _____

Commit your actions to the Lord, and your plans will succeed.

—Proverbs 16:3

ACKNOWLEDGEMENTS

First and foremost, my grateful acknowledgement to God for his grace and mercy, and good plans for my life.

My sincere thanks to Katie Brazelton, Ph.D., author, teacher, mentor, and founder of Life Purpose Coaching Centers International® for always speaking truth in love and suggesting I write my own coaching process—which turned out to be *Your HeartSong Journey*.

Thank you to Ladies in Prayer (affectionately known as LIPS). Our time spent in prayer humbles, guides, emboldens, and holds me accountable. How grateful I am to see each one of you bravely living your HeartSong.

To my three grown kids and their loves, Madison and Doug, Logan and Lindsey, and Hudson and Laura, my deep appreciation for your love and example of what it is to grow in Christ...and for your hugs. You inspire me.

Finally, to my ever-loving husband and forever-best friend, Walt, who patiently watched, waited, and prayed me through to the very last page. Thank you for playing the *giving game* with me. Somehow, you always seem to win.

You're Invited

You're invited to share with Gail what God has revealed about your sacred worth, his dreams, and his purpose for you on your personal journey through these pages. And, if you'd like to....

- Learn more about Gail's online *Breakthrough Coaching* small group,
- Request a complimentary 1-1 *Coaching Discovery* call, or
- Invite Gail to speak at your event....

please email gail@gailarmatys.com with your story and request, or contact her at www.gailarmatys.com.

ENDNOTES

Step One

1. Katie Brazelton, *Conversations on Purpose for Women: 10 Appointments That Will Help You Discover God's Plan for Your Life* (Grand Rapids, MI: Zondervan, 2005), 26-27
2. Gary D. Chapman, *The 5 Love Languages: The Secret of Love That Lasts.* (Chicago, IL: Northfield Publishing, 2015).
3. Max Lucado, *He Chose the Nails: What God Did to Win Your Heart* (Nashville: Thomas Nelson, 2017), 65.

Step Two

1. Raymond Edman, *They Found the Secret* (Grand Rapids, MI: Zondervan Pub. House, 1984), 46.
2. Katie Brazelton, *Conversations on Purpose for Women: 10 Appointments That Will Help You Discover God's Plan for Your Life* (Grand Rapids, MI: Zondervan, 2005), 39.
3. Carol S. Dweck, *Mindset: The New Psychology of Success* (New York: Random House, 2016), 6.
4. Carol S. Dweck, *Mindset: The New Psychology of Success* (New York: Random House, 2016), 7.
5. Ann Voskamp, *One Thousand Gifts: A Dare to Live Fully Right Where You Are* (S.l.: Zondervan, 2015), book jacket cover.
6. Caroline Leaf, *Switch on Your Brain: The Key to Peak Happiness, Thinking, and Health* (S.l.: Baker Book House, 2018), 20.
7. Katie Brazelton and Shelley Leith, *Character Makeover: 40 Days with a Life Coach to Create the Best You* (Grand Rapids, MI: Zondervan, 2008), 137.
8. VIA Survey, Via Institute on Character, © 2019 VIA Institute on Character, https://www.viacharacter.org/survey/account/register
9. Rick Warren, *The Purpose Driven Life* (Chagrin Falls, OH: Zondervan, 2006), 21.

10. Diane Langberg, *Suffering and the Heart of God: How Trauma Destroys and Christ Restores* (Greensboro, NC: New Growth Press, 2015), 175.
11. Katie Brazelton, *Conversations on Purpose for Women: 10 Appointments That Will Help You Discover God's Plan for Your Life* (Grand Rapids, MI: Zondervan, 2005), 58.
12. *How to Forgive*, excerpts from a sermon by Corrie Ten Boom, www.sermonindex.net, https://www.youtube.com/watch?v=3cfp51vLZb4
13. Charles R. Swindoll, https://www.insight.org

Step Three

1. Jeff Jernigan, Ph.D., LPC, BCPPC, Life Purpose Coaching Centers, International®, https://lifepurposecoachingcenters.com
2. Spiritual Gifts Test©, 2019, https://spiritualgiftstest.com
3. Vivek Haldar, blog.vivekhaldar.com
4. This I Believe (The Creed) Hillsong Worship, Hillsong Music Publishing© 2014, https://www.youtube.com/watch?v=FtUNQpu2b7Q
5. *Mirriam-Webster*, © 2019 Mirriam-Webster, Incorporated, https://www.merriam-webster.com/dictionary/surrender
6. Kyle Idleman, *Not a Fan*, © 2011, (Grand Rapids, MI:Zondervan), 152.
7. James Allen, *As a Man Thinketh*, (New York, NY: First Jeremy P. Tarcher/ Penguin, 2008), 29.

ABOUT THE AUTHOR

Gail Armatys, M.S. pursues her *HeartSong* guiding others to conquer what holds them back so they can live the new lives they deep down crave and have been given. She coaches, writes, and speaks from a faith-based and life-purpose perspective on subjects of self-worth, character strengths and development, overcoming life-diminishing fears, doubts, habits, and thoughts, and creating life-success strategies for personal and professional growth.

Having known what it is to live with a low self-esteem, find comfort in an eating disorder, experience divorce, feel empty, and be dissatisfied with a life defined by most as very successful, Gail uses her experiences, education, and training to help others get unstuck, experience transformation, and know and live their calling.

Prior to coaching, and for nearly thirty years, Gail was co-founder and administrator of a successful private college, helping staff and graduates meet their career goals. Her Master's Degree is in Human Development and the Family, and she is a trained mediator, and a Professional Certified Life Coach. Gail and her husband, Walt, have been married for twenty-eight years and moved from their home state of Nebraska to Texas long ago. They're especially grateful to live near their three amazing adult children and growing family.